D0373638

There's a Japanese game called Atchi Muite Hoi (Look That Way) where one player has to turn their head in one of the four directions while the other player points with a finger, hoping to guess the same direction.
Well, I've invented a secret weapon called Atchi Muite Hoi 3-D that has ten directions instead. If a kid ever challenges you to Atchi Muite Hoi, use this method to childishly avoid losing!!
Here comes Volume 82!!!

-Eiichiro Oda, 2016

Eiichiro Oda began his manga career at the age of 17, when his one-shot cowboy manga **Wanted!** won second place in the coveted Tezuka manga awards. Oda went on to work as an assistant to some of the biggest manga artists in the industry, including Nobuhiro Watsuki, before winning the Hop Step Award for new artists. His pirate adventure **One Piece**, which debuted in **Weekly Shonen Jump** in 1997, quickly became one of the most popular manga in Japan.

ONE PIECE VOL. 82
NEW WORLD PART 22

SHONEN JUMP Manga Edition

STORY AND ART BY EIICHIRO ODA

Translation/Stephen Paul
Touch-up Art & Lettering/Vanessa Satone
Design/Yukiko Whitley
Editor/Alexis Kirsch

ONE PIECE © 1997 by Eiichiro Oda. All rights reserved.
First published in Japan in 1997 by SHUEISHA Inc., Tokyo.
English translation rights arranged by SHUEISHA Inc.

The stories, characters and incidents mentioned in this publication are entirely fictional.

No portion of this book may be reproduced or transmitted in any form or by any means without written permission from the copyright holders.

Printed in the U.S.A.

Published by VIZ Media, LLC
P.O. Box 77010
San Francisco, CA 94107

10 9 8 7 6 5 4 3 2 1
First printing, May 2017

www.viz.com

ONE PIECE
Vol. 82
THE WORLD IS RESTLESS
STORY AND ART BY
EIICHIRO ODA

The Straw Hat Crew

Tony Tony Chopper

After researching powerful medicine in Birdie Kingdom, he reunited with the rest of the crew.

Ship's Doctor, Bounty: 100 berries

Monkey D. Luffy

A young man who dreams of becoming the Pirate King. After training with Rayleigh, he and his crew head for the New World!

Captain, Bounty: 500 million berries

Nico Robin

She spent her time in Baltigo with the leader of the Revolutionary Army: Luffy's father, Dragon.

Archeologist, Bounty: 130 million berries

Roronoa Zolo

He swallowed his pride and asked to be trained by Mihawk on Gloom Island before reuniting with the rest of the crew.

Fighter, Bounty: 320 million berries

Franky

He modified himself in Future Land Baldimore and turned himself into Armored Franky before reuniting with the rest of the crew.

Shipwright, Bounty: 94 million berries

Nami

She studied the weather of the New World on the small Sky Island Weatheria, a place where weather is studied as a science.

Navigator, Bounty: 66 million berries

Brook

After being captured and used as a freak show by the Longarm Tribe, he became a famous rock star called "Soul King" Brook.

Musician, Bounty: 83 million berries

Usopp

He trained under Heracles at the Bowin Islands to become the King of Snipers.

Sniper, Bounty: 200 million berries

Shanks

One of the Four Emperors. Waits for Luffy in the "New World," the second half of the Grand Line.

Captain of the Red-Haired Pirates

Sanji

After fighting the New Kama Karate masters in the Kamabakka Kingdom, he returned to the crew.

Cook, Bounty: 177 million berries

kingdom from his control. After an exhausting battle, they remove Doflamingo from the land he torments! Luffy's team then sails ahead to catch up and regroup with Nami's team on the island of Zou. When they get there, it turns out that Kaido's crony Jack has already leveled the city. The minks were hiding the samurai Jack sought, but to them, the Kozuki Clan are like family that they would never sell out, even if their country fell to ruin. The crew is stunned by this heartfelt loyalty... Meanwhile, Sanji's family background is revealed, and events take a sudden, unexpected turn!

Trafalgar Law

Captain of the Heart Pirates

Caesar Clown

Former Govt Scientist

Wano Kingdom

Foxfire Kin'emon

Samurai of Wano

Evening Shower Kanjuro

Samurai of Wano

Momonosuke

Kin'emon's Son

Mokomo Dukedom

Duke Dogstorm

King of the Day

Full-Power Shishilian (Lion Mink)

Captain of the Dogstorm Musketeers

Wanda (Dog Mink)

Battlebeast Tribe

Carrot (Bunny Mink)

Battlebeast Tribe

The Cat Viper

Spirit of the Whale Forest, King of the Night

Treetop Pedro (Jaguar Mink)

Leader of the Guardians

Roddy (Bull Mink)

Guardian of the Whale Forest

BB (Gorilla Mink)

Guardian of the Whale Forest

Animal Kingdom Pirates

Kaido, King of the Beasts

Captain of the Animal Kingdom Pirates

Jack the Drought

Lead Performer of the A.K. Pirates

Big Mom Pirates

Baron Tamago

Fighter, Big Mom Pirates

Pekoms

Fighter, Big Mom Pirates

Capone "Gang" Bege

Captain of the Firetank Pirates

Story

After two years of hard training, the Straw Hat pirates are back together, first at the Sabaody Archipelago and then through Fish-Man Island to their next stage: the New World!!

The crew happens across Trafalgar Law on the island of Punk Hazard. At his suggestion, they form a new pirate alliance that seeks to take down one of the Four Emperors. The group infiltrates the kingdom of Dressrosa in an attempt to take down Doflamingo, Kaido's trading partner, and find themselves in a battle to liberate the

Vol. 82

THE WORLD IS RESTLESS

CONTENTS

Chapter 817: Raizo of the Mist	011
Chapter 818: Inside the Whale	029
Chapter 819: Momonosuke, Heir to the Kozuki Clan	047
Chapter 820: Cats and Dogs Have a History	065
Chapter 821: Understood	082
Chapter 822: Descending the Elephant	103
Chapter 823: The World Is Restless	121
Chapter 824: Playing Pirates	138
Chapter 825: Comic Strip	159
Chapter 826: 0 and 4	173
Chapter 827: Totto Land	191

ONE PIECE

Hereafter, the 82nd volume will start.

GOLD
ワンピース フィルム ゴールド
ONE PIECE FILM

vol.82

ONE PIECE

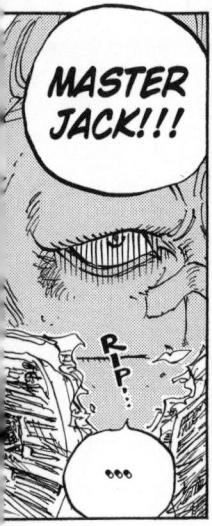

CHAPTER 817: RAIZO OF THE MIST

OBSERVE !!!
FWUP!
DO
Om!!
IT IS JUST AS RAIZO BEARS.
YOUR GRACE! BOSS!
YES, THAT IS IT!
!!
...OF THE KOZUKI CLAN!!
DA-DOOm!!
THE OFFICIAL CREST...

IT COULDN'T BE HELPED... IT WAS A SECRET FROM US TOO...
AND HERE WE WERE WORRIED ABOUT A CLASH WITH THE MINKS!
SO THEY KNEW EACH OTHER ALL ALONG...
KOE-ZOOKY?
CHATTER
CHATTER

MAYBE THE BOND BETWEEN THEM IS MUCH DEEPER THAN WE REALIZE.
THEY SAID THAT DOGGY AND KITTY HAVE THE CREST TOO!

BUT WE NEEDED TO WAIT HERE, BASED ON THE PACT OF THAT DAY.
WELL, IT WAS A CLOSE CALL.
EXACTLY!! WE KNEW WE COULD MEET YOUGARA AGAIN!!

IT IS A SURPRISE TO ME THAT YOU ARE BOTH STILL ALIVE!!!
I'LL BE HONEST, DOGSTORM AND CAT VIPER!!

PLEASE, YOU TWO, STOP!!
SO I TOOK OVER THE CONVERSATION INSTEAD!!!
OH YEAH?! WELL, I THOUGHT HE'D GET SICK TALKIN' TO YOUGARA!!
HEY, MONSTER CAT! I WAS TALKING TO KIN'EMON JUST NOW!!
OUR LONG-AWAITED VISITOR HAS FINALLY ARRIVED...
NAH, YOU TUCK YOUR TAIL AND SCRAM!!!
YOUGARA ARE FINISHED HERE!! BEGONE!!
RAH
MROWW!!
GRRR!!
AAA
AHH

ER, WELL...
WHY WOULD YOU FIGHT TO THE DEATH LIKE THAT?!
YOU WERE SUCH CLOSE FRIENDS BEFORE!
I FORBID YOU TO FIGHT AGAIN!!!

?!
CAT VIPER, DOG-STORM!! STOP THIS FIGHTING !!!

IF FATHER SAW YOU ACTING LIKE THIS, HE WOULD BE VERY SAD!!!
ESPECIALLY IF WHAT HAPPENED TO FATHER IS THE CAUSE!!!

BUT KIN'EMON'S RIGHT THERE.
"FATHER" ...?
?
MOMO?
LORD ODEN...
...!!
FWOMP!!
I AM ASHAMED, LORD MOMONOSUKE !!
FORGIVE US!!!
YER RIGHT, OF COURSE!!
IT IS AS LORD MOMONO-SUKE SAYS!!
?!!
THE BOSS IS BOWING HIS HEAD TO THAT BOY!
YOUR GRACE ?!!
HUH ?!!
MURMUR!!
COULD HE BE--

WHAT?!!
IN FACT, LORD MOMONOSUKE AND I ARE NOT FATHER AND SON!!!
FORGIVE US FOR DECEIVING YOU!!
!!
LORD KOZUKI MOMONO-SUKE!!!
STANDING BEFORE YOU IS THE HEIR...
...TO KOZUKI ODEN, GREAT DAIMYO OF KURI IN THE LAND OF WANO!!!
DAIMYO OF KURI, WANO (HEIR) KOZUKI MOMONOSUKE
IF THEY ARE THE FAMILY'S VASSALS, HE MUST BE A VERY POWERFUL LORD INDEED.
SO MOMO'S SOME KINDA BIG SHOT?
FORGIVE US FOR NOT REALIZING!!
LORD ODEN'S SON!!
HEIR OF THE KOZUKI CLAN!!
HHH

DA-DOOm!!
BUT REVEALING HIS IDENTITY ON OUR TRAVELS WOULD BRING DOWN ENEMIES UPON US...
...SO WE ENACTED A RUSE AND PRETENDED TO BE FATHER AND SON!!
MEANING THAT TO US, INCLUDING DOGSTORM AND CAT VIPER...
...HE IS OUR LIEGE!!

I AM ACTUALLY VERY IMPORTANT!!
SORRY FOR LYING TO YOU.
THEY LOOK SO ALIKE.
SO YOU'RE NOT A FAMILY?!
A VERY IMP PERVERT INDEED!!
I SAID VERY IMPORTANT!
DEH HEH HEH♡

I DID TRUST YOU TO KEEP OUR SECRET, BUT I MISSED THE RIGHT OPPORTUNITY TO REVEAL ALL.

...MEANS THE REST OF US HAVE TO CHANGE HOW WE ACT?! YOU STUPID JERK!!
NO WAY! HOW COME YOU BEIN' SOME FANCY GUY...
LORD MOMONO-SUKE!!

WHAT DO YOU MEAN, SO WHAT?! GROVEL WHEN YOU SPEAK TO ME, LUFFY!!
SO WHAT ?!

YOU CANNOT EXPECT PIRATES TO HAVE MANNERS.
THERE THEY GO AGAIN... WELL, THEY ARE OUR SAVIORS...
AT LEAST IT IS A GOOD DISTRACTION FOR HIM, PERHAPS?
A WARRIOR IS AFRAID OF NOTHING, YOU BRAZEN LOUT!!!
YOU'RE JUST A WIMP WHO'S AFRAID OF HEIGHTS!!
GYAA
BOP BOP
GYAA
RAHH
GET AWAY FROM HER, LORD MOMONOSUKE!! YOU WICKED BRAT!!!
BA-M!
HEY.
NOW, NOW. THERE, THERE.♡
CURSES! OWAMI, LUFFY IS THE MOST BEASTLY MAN!!
BOOF♡
AND IT'S ONLY BEEN A FEW MONTHS SINCE THEN.
BWA HA HA HA
GYAA
RAHH
I SUPPOSE THE LIVELINESS OF THOSE FOLKS HAS BEEN A BLESSING TO HIM...
DON'T YOU DARE !!!
...THEN I SUPPOSE HIS CASTLE HAS A LOT OF TREASURE.♡
OH, MOMO? IF YOUR FATHER IS A GREAT LORD...
SQUISH♡

I MIGHT SHARE WORDS WITH YOUGARA BUT NOT MY SYMPATHIES!!
ONLY FOR THE SAKE OF OUR LIEGE!!
...IT WILL ONLY PAIN LORD MOMONO-SUKE.
IF WE LET THIS DRAG ON AND ON...
LET'S HAVE A CEASE-FIRE, CAT!!
DO
DO
DO!!
IT'S A MIRACLE !!!
OHHH
OOOH !!!
SNAG
!!
I WOULDN'T HAVE IT ANY OTHER WAY!!!
I THINK I'M CRYING!!
YAHOO !!!
...
THE TWO KINGS HAVE MADE PEACE!!!
RAAAAAA
AH!!
...BROUGHT TOGETHER BY THE POWER OF KOZUKI!!!
THE KING OF DAY AND KING OF NIGHT...
RAAAA
AAA
AH
.....!!
!!

GUARDIANS' DWELLING

THIS IS WHERE RAIZO IS?!

...AND IT'LL GETCHA TO THE TOP.

WE'RE GONNA CLIMB THE WHALE.

JUST REMEMBER THE ORDER OF VINES TO CROSS...

DO

YA!!

YEAH. THAT REMINDED ME OF HIM TOO...
THERE WAS ANOTHER MAN WHO SAID MUCH THE SAME THING.
YOUR DISPOSITION IS SIMILAR TO LORD ODEN'S...
THE CLOSER TO THE WHALE, THE LOUDER THE "VOICE" I HEAR.
...
THERE'S AN ENTRANCE HERE?!
YA'D NEVER KNOW IT.
AND HIDDEN DOORS AFTER.
THERE YOU ARE, CAT VIPER!!!
YAHOO!! WHERE'S THE NINJA ?!!
WELL, HERE WE ARE!!
NINJA, NINJA!
NINJ...
NINJA !!
I HEAR SCREAMING FROM BELOW!!
KAARGH
THESE STAIRS LAST AWHILE.
WATCH YOUR STEP.

IF YOU ARE LYING TO ME, THEN KNOW THAT YOU HAVE EARNED THE WRATH OF RAIZO!!!
THEY TOLD ME THE COUNTRY WAS SAFE...BUT IS IT TRUE?!!
EVERY-ONE WHO BROUGHT MY FOOD WAS INJURED!!!
WHY DID YOU NOT HAND ME TO YOUR FOES?!!
KAAAH !!!
?!!
NINJA OF WANO
RAIZO OF THE MIST
GO NG!!
...WHAT I EX-PECTED !!!
WHAAAT ?!! THAT IS NOT...

RAIZOOO!!
WHO GOES THERE?!!
KAH !!!
WHA--?!
IS THAT...THE KOZUKI CLAN CREST?!
YOU ARE ALL WELL!!
AND YOU!!
LORD MOMONO-SUKE!!
OHHH!! KIN'EMON!! KANJURO !!
THE CREST HAS BEEN HERE FOR CENTURIES.
YEP! IT'S A PONEGLIFF!!
I'VE NEVER SEEN ONE SO...RED!
AND... THAT STONE?!
CHATTER
CHATTER
AND I KNOW ABOUT YOUGARA, NICO ROBIN!! I'VE HEARD THAT OHARA DECIPHERED THOSE RUNES.

WHAT IS WITH YOU PEOPLE?! WHY DO YOU STARE AT ME SO INTENTLY?!
HMM
HMM
WHAT? HOW RUDE!
ARE YOU REALLY A NINJA?
YES... MAY I?
B'BNP
B'BNP
OF COURSE.
IT HAS A DIFFERENT USAGE, APPARENTLY. CAN YOU READ IT?
WHY IS IT COLORED RED?
I WANNA SEE THE FIRE ELEMENT!!
SHOW US THE EARTH ELEMENT TECHNIQUES!
DO SOME NINPO ARTS!!
STAND UNDER A WATER-FALL!
THROW SOME SHURIKEN FOR US!!
PIRATES ?!!
WATER ELEMENT FOR ME!!
THEY HAVE A STORM OF REQUESTS!!!
GYAA
RATTT
THESE ARE THE STRAW HAT PIRATES.
WHY, YOU ARE MAKING ME BLUSH !!!
...LOVES NINJA!!!
EVERY MAN...
IT AIN'T BECAUSE WE'RE PIRATES!!
AND WHY WOULD PIRATES WANT SUCH A THING...?
?!

HOLD A SCROLL IN YOUR MOUTH AND SAY "NIN, NIN"!!!
HIDE BEHIND THE CEILING AND GET STABBED BY A SPEAR.
SHOW ME YOUR DOPPEL-GÄNGER TECH-NIQUE.
TRAIN YOUR SKILLS BY JUMPING OVER EVER-GROWING BAMBOO STALKS!
HAVE YOU EVER GONE OUT WITH A KUNOICHI, A FEMALE NINJA?!
...!!!
WHAAAT?!!
THOSE NINJA ARE A FIGMENT OF YOUR IMAGINA-TION!!!
NINJA DO NOT SAY "NIN, NIN"!!
KAA—H!!
DON'T PUSH YOUR STEREO-TYPES ON ME !!!
SILENCE, ALREADY !!!
?!!
ONE WHO LIVES IN THE SHADOWS DOES NOT SIMPLY DISPLAY HIS SKILLS TO OTHERS!
LISTEN! A SHINOBI IS THE MASTER OF A QUIET BUT STRONG HEART!!!
YES...A FIGURE THAT HAS NEVER WON ME POINTS WITH THE KUNOICHI--
THEN WHAT MAKES YOU A NINJA?! WITH A FIGURE LIKE THAT!
DON'T BRING THAT UP!!!
...
NINJUTSU ARE NOT PARTY TRICKS THAT...
BUMMER

SMOKE ESCAPE TECH-NIQUE !!!
NINPO !!!
WHUP !!
?!!
BWO mm!!
KAAAH !!!
HE DIS-APPEARED!!!
WHAAA
I HAVE NOT!!
HE--
DORORON!
OH!!
AND HERE!!
DORON!
AND HERE.
DORON!
AND HERE.
WHAAAT!!! HE MULTI-PLIED!! COULD THIS BE--
DORON!!
AAAAH !!
I AM RIGHT HERE.
DORON!

YOU WANT TO KNOW IF I'M A NINJA?!!
SHU SHU SHU
TATATUM!!
FLOWER SHURIKEN !!!
WUP WUP
COOL !!!
NINPO: SHADOW CLONE JUTSU!!!
...BUT I'M INVINCIBLE AS A NINJA!!!
BA-BA-BA!!
I MAY BE INVISIBLE TO WOMEN...
WHOA !!
KA KA KAKA!!
*THE SHURIKEN SPELL OUT "SHINOBI."
DORON
...IS UPON THE SCENE!!!
RAIZO OF THE MIST...
KATKATKAN!!
NIN!! NIN!!!
RAIZOOO !!!

(Takahisa Fujimoto, Nara)

A: Hello there. I suppose we'll get started with our question and ans—

Q: I recognize that face… You're Eiichiro Oda, aren't ya? I hear you're having trouble with your SBS segment getting hijacked... So you tried to line up at the SBS arena first thing in the morning. Nice try, pal!!! I lined up three days ago. So **I'm** gonna say the words…

"Let's start the SBS!!"

--Komashu

A: Whoaaaa!!
I have to wait a hundred years to try again?!

Q: Oda Sensei, I've got big trouble. Akainu is standing right behind me. What should I do?

--Junpei T.

A: First, stay calm. I'm going to show you the pose that will allow you to get past Akainu. Shape your mouth into a "3" sign, look up and to the left, and start whistling. This will help you slip past most major threats: Bears, Ghosts, you name it.

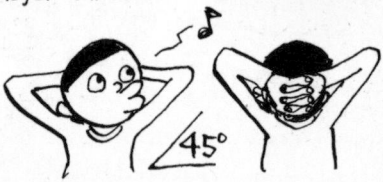

Chapter 818: INSIDE THE WHALE

DECKS OF THE WORLD, 500-MILLION-MAN ARC,
VOL. 11: "BALTIGO"

DON'T BE PRE-POSTEROUS !!
YOU ONLY SAW MY NINJUTSU THROUGH COINCIDENCE !!
GYAA !!
ENOUGH WITH THE "NIN-NIN"!!
NIN-NIN!
NIN-NIN!
COINCI-DENCE?! YOU GAVE US A SHOW!!
ARE YOU GUYS CRYING?
HMM?
OH!!
OO...OH!!
WHEN I FIRST ARRIVED HERE...
...IT WAS NOT LIKE THIS!!!
THE CITY AND RIVERS WERE PRISTINE!!!

FORGIVE ME!!!
ON MY HONOR...I WILL WORK TO MAKE THIS RIGHT!!!
SNIFF
HICK
FORGIVE ME...

...

.....!!
...

LOOKS LIKE THE READING OF THE STONE IS COMPLETE.
!
HEY! YOUGARA !!
COME INSIDE THE WHALE!!

MEN OF WANO DO NOT CRY!!!
IT'S JUST...

IT WAS LIVELY AND BUZZING WITH ACTIVITY!!
THE COUNTRY WAS ALIVE!!!
THOSE CRAZY MINKS-- LOYAL TO A FAULT!!

I'M PRETTY SURE THIS CAN BE USED TO IDENTIFY A LOCATION, ROBIN!!
THIS IS WHAT WAS WRITTEN ON THE PONEGLIFF?
YES, I CAN DEFINITELY USE THIS TO DRAW A NAVAL MAP!
WHAT DO YOU THINK, NAMI?
THAT RED STONE IS CALLED A ROAD PONEGLIFF!!
!!

...AND WHY THE GUARDIANS ARE NECESSARY TA PROTECT IT!!!
THIS IS WHY THE WHALE FOREST IS HELD TA BE SACRED...
...TO RAFTEL, THE FINAL ISLAND?!!
YOU MEAN ...
B-BMP
B-BMP
PRECISELY !!
WHAT ?!!
HOWEVER ...
IT IS MEANT TO SERVE AS A GUIDE TO THE PLACE THE MOST POWERFUL MEN ON THE SEA SEEK!!
THE END POINT OF THE GRAND LINE!!!
?!!

RAFTEL?!!
HOW-EVER!!
WAIT, WAIT, SLOW DOWN. HOWEVER!!
WHAAAT?! THAT THING SAYS WHERE RAFTEL IS?!
THAT'S THE KING OF THE PIRATES!!!
THAT'S THE END GOAL!!!
GYAAAA
...BUT FOUR!!
?!!
THERE IS NOT ONE RED ROAD PONEGLIFF IN THE WORLD...

YES, THIS STONE MARKS A POINT...
...BUT THAT POINT IS NOT RAFTEL.
SIMILARLY, THE OTHER THREE RED STONES...
NO!! LET HIM FINISH THE STORY!!
WHAAAT?! THERE ARE FOUR RAFTELS?!
WHACK!!
AAAA
...IT WILL NATURALLY APPEAR IN THE MIDDLE OF THEM!!!
...AND YOU CONNECT THE FOUR POINTS ON A MAP...
WHEN YOU KNOW THEM ALL...
...CONTAIN THE COORDI-NATES FOR OTHER POINTS!!
GR
BOOM!!
RRG
RAFTEL !!!
DO
OH!!
THE LOCATION OF THE FINAL ISLAND, WHICH FOR CENTURIES...
...HAS ONLY BEEN REACHED BY THE KING OF THE PIRATES AND HIS CREW...

SO IT'S FINALLY TIME...
THE PLACE WHERE WE MIGHT FIND...
...OR MIGHT NOT FIND...
...THE ONE PIECE!!
SHIVER
SHIVER
AWRIGHT!! WE'RE GONNA GO SEARCHING !!!
DON'T WORRY, I'LL GO GET SANJI BACK IN A JIFFY!!
WHERE ARE YOU GONNA SEARCH?! THE WORLD'S A BIG PLACE!!!
IF YOU HEAD FOR WHOLE CAKE ISLAND WITH PEKOMS...
...THEN YER ON THE RIGHT TRACK!
?!
YAAA

...AND KAIDO, KING OF THE BEASTS!!!
THE EMPERORS OF THE SEA, BIG MOM...
?!!
DA-DO-!!

WHAAAAAAAAT?!!
EACH OF THEM OWNS...
GOOD TO KNOW!!
SO WE JUST GOTTA STEAL 'EM.
...ONE OF THE OTHER TWO RED STONES!!
AAAAAAGH

...MAKES ME ALMOST PEE MY PANTS IN FRIGHT!!
DON'T MAKE IT SOUND SO EASY!! I COULD IGNORE IT AS THE DISTANT FUTURE UNTIL NOW, BUT THE THOUGHT OF FIGHTING THEM...
...SO WHO CARES ?!!
SO WHAT?! I'M GONNA WHOOP 'EM ANYWAY...
OH GOSH... MY VISION JUST WENT BLACK...
YEAH, I'LL PEE MYSELF!! DON'T THINK I WON'T!!!
HURP!

JUST MAKE A SIMPLE PRINT OF THE MESSAGE.

NOBODY GOES LUGGIN' THESE HUGE THINGS AROUND!!

THE THING IS, YA DON'T EVEN NEED...

...TA ***STEAL*** A PONEGLIFF.

?

...

HARUMF

!!

BA—M!!

OH, OF COURSE !!!

SO JUST SNEAK IN, MAKE A QUICK COPY...

BEFORE ANYONE REALIZES IT, SLIP OFF TO RAFTEL...

...AND BOOM! YOU'RE THE PIRATE KING!!!

ANYONE INTERESTED IN THE ***VOID CENTURY*** IS OUT THERE COLLECTIN' PRINTS OF THE PONEGLIFFS...

!

...NICO ROBIN.

MORE IMPORTANTLY, I'M WORRIED FER YOURGARA SAKE...

WHAT ARE YOU SO DISAPPOINTED ABOUT?!

DAAA!!

GYAA

RAHH

...BUT NONE O' THEM'S ABLE TO DECIPHER THE MEANING!!

WHO CARES ABOUT BEING MANLY?! YOU'D RATHER WAGE WAR?!

...BIG PLAYERS FROM ALL OVER THE WORLD WILL BE AFTER YOUGARA.
BUT WHEN THE TIME COMES THAT THEY WANNA KNOW THE TRUTH...

...I'VE GOT VERY POWERFUL FRIENDS WHO WILL PROTECT ME.
!
I DON'T MIND. AFTER ALL...
HEE HEE HEE

...
AFTER ROBIN?!!
PAUSE

MROW-ROW-ROW!! HEARTY COMPANIONS TO HAVE!!
RATI GYAA
BY THE WAY...HOW DO YOU KNOW SO MUCH ABOUT THE PONEGLIFFS?

I WON'T LET ANYONE LAY A FINGER ON ROBIN!!!
YOU CAN'T JUST RELY ON ME LIKE THAT... HWACHA! HOCHAA!!
WHOA, WHOA, YOU'RE GONNA MAKE ME BLUSH, TALKING LIKE THAT!! WHY, I OUGHTA POUND ANYONE IN MY WAY!!
AND IF THEY DO, I'LL TAKE THEIR LIFE AND THEIR MONEY!!
NOPE
NOPE
NOPE

WELL... YOU MIND IF I TELL THEM, DOG?!
BUT THAT TOO, IS...
...BEGAN TO DEVELOP AN INTEREST IN THE STONES.
THAT STORY STARTS LONG IN THE PAST, WHEN OUR LORD KOZUKI ODEN...
...
TELL THEM ANYTHING YOU WISH!
I DO NOT MIND. THERE IS NO NEED TO HIDE SECRETS FROM THEM!!
BO
OM!!
...
GLANCE..
EVEN NOW, THEIR SKILL WITH ROCK IS UNPARALLELED.
...HAS BEEN A LINE OF STONEMASONS, CUTTING AND CARVING STONE.
FOR GENERATIONS, THE KOZUKI CLAN OF WANO...
STONE-MASONS ?!
WHADDAYOU MEAN, YOU DON'T MIND?! TRYIN' TO ACT ALL BOSSY AGAIN!!
BO-ZK
BO-ZK
I CANNOT HELP BEING BOSSY, YOU CRUDE LOUT! I AM IMPORTANT!!

THE PONEGLIFFS !!!
...THE KOZUKI CLAN CREATED INDESTRUCTIBLE STONE DOCUMENTS.
THAT'S RIGHT. EIGHT CENTURIES IN THE PAST...
?!!!

WHAAAAAAT?!!
...
WHA
AAAA
IHT

I DID NOT MAKE THEM!!
YOU?!
THOSE STONES THAT ROBIN'S BEEN SEARCHING FOR?!
IT WAS MY LONG-DISTANT ANCESTORS!!

THE CLAN THAT CREATED THE PONEGLIFFS SCATTERED ALL OVER THE WORLD?!

AND THE ONLY THING THAT WAS PASSED DOWN WAS THE WAY TO READ THE ANCIENT RUNES.
YOU MUST READ THE STONES TO LEARN THE CONTENTS.
THEY DID NOT PASS DOWN THE INFORMATION!
SO DO YOU KNOW WHAT'S WRITTEN ON THEM?!
?!

YES. LORD ODEN IS...
WANO... IS...!!

CUT SHORT...? YOU MEAN...
MOMONO-SUKE'S FATHER IS...?!

...THE PROCESS WAS CUT SHORT IN HIS FATHER KOZUKI ODEN'S GENERATION...
...!!

...BEFORE LORD MOMONO-SUKE COULD RECEIVE THE TEACHINGS...
BUT MOST TRAGICALLY ...

...!!!
HNG!!!
HIC
I AM ODEN!! I WAS BORN TO BOIL!!!
DRIP
FFFH ...!!

HEY, IT'S FINE!! YOU DON'T HAVE TO EXPLAIN IF YOU DON'T WANT TO...
BY THE SHOGUN OF WANO AND THE PIRATE KAIDO!!!
LORD ODEN... WAS PUT TO DEATH!!!
?!!!
DA-DO OH!!
WHAT ?!!

KAIDO ?!!
HE GAVE HIS LIFE MOST ADMIRABLY...
...TO SAVE THE LIVES OF ALL HIS SERVANTS!!
KAIDO...?!
KAIDO, EMPEROR OF THE SEA...
...AND HIS ANIMAL KINGDOM PIRATES...
...ARE IN WANO!!!
?!!

...BEING CAPTURED AND CHASED AND STUFF?
SNIFF...
DOES IT HAVE SOMETHING TO DO WITH YOU GUYS...
YOU DON'T HAVE TO ANSWER THIS QUESTION, BUT...
WHAT DID YOUR BOSS DO TO GET EXECUTED?
LORD KOZUKI ODEN...
THE OLD DAIMYO...
KAIDO IS ATTEMPT-ING...TO PRY INFORMATION OUT OF US.
YES... AS YOU SUSPECT, HIS CRIME WAS GRIEVOUS...
?!
...TO RAFTEL, THE FINAL ISLAND!!
AND IT WAS THERE THAT HE LEARNED THE SECRET OF THE WORLD!!!
WHAT ?!!
...RODE WITH THE KING OF THE PIRATES, GOL D. ROGER...
DOOM!!

SBS Question Corner

(Hayato Asami, Kanagawa)

Q: Oda Sensei! Please tell us the hobbies of the Worst Generation!

--K.S.9

A:

Luffy
Adventuring, parties

Zolo
Training, booze

Law
Wandering, collecting commemorative coins

Kid
Listening to music, weapon collecting

Apoo
DJ-ing, surfing

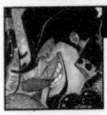

Bege
Contemplating art, board games

Hawkins
Interior design, bathing

Drake
Loves reptiles, astrophysics

Bonney
Eating, Jenga

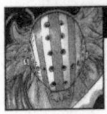

Killer
Drums, cooking

Urouge
Booze, debauchery, mountain climbing

Blackbeard
Gambling, studying history

That's about it.

Q: In the Grand Ship Collection line of figurines, there's one simply titled "Trafalgar Law's Submarine." Doesn't it have a catchy name like the *Thousand Sunny?*

--Aspiring Heart Pirates Member

©Eiichiro Oda/Shueisha - Fuji TV - Toei Animation

A: Oh, they put one of those out, did they? It's called the *Polar Tang*. It's hard to work the names into the story, so these things slip through.

Q: Gorilla is yummy.
I like Lassen's dolphin paintings.

--Taro Sasaki

A: Thank you for your letter.

Chapter 819: MOMONOSUKE, HEIR TO THE KOZUKI CLAN

DECKS OF THE WORLD, 500-MILLION-MAN ARC,
VOL. 12: "FUTURE LAND BALDIMORE"

...WITH GOLD ROGER ?!!
MOMONOSUKE'S DAD WENT TO RAFTEL...
WHAAAAAAAT..!!!
DO
Om!
...!!
SNIFF..
...WAS PART OF THE KING OF THE PIRATES' CREW?!
YOUR DAD...
WE LEARNED ABOUT EVERYTHING THAT OCCURRED...
YES, WE KNOW.
JUST LIKE RAYLEIGH...
A MAN WHO LEARNED THE SECRETS OF THE WORLD!!

...WERE TRYING TO LEARN THESE "SECRETS OF THE WORLD" OR WHATEVER...
...FROM YOU GUYS, SINCE YOU WERE HIS SERVANTS.
I GET IT. SO YOU'RE SAYING...
...DOFLAMINGO AND CAESAR, WORKING AS AN EXTENSION OF KAIDO...

YES...NOT THAT WE WOULD SAY ANYTHING IF WE DID!!
WE KNOW NOTHING !!!
BUT LORD ODEN MADE CERTAIN NOT TO BURDEN US WITH ANY SECRETS!

THAT IS THE CASE...

LORD ODEN LEFT US BUT ONE MESSAGE BEFORE HIS DEATH!!

WHICH LEAVES US ONLY ONE CHOICE...
BUT WHETHER WE KNOW OR NOT, OUR PURSUERS NEVER CEASE!
TO FIGHT !!!

OPEN WANO'S BORDERS!!!
DA-DO OM!!
NOW THAT WE LIVE WITH THIS TERRIBLE SHAME OVER OUR HEADS...
...OUR ONLY CHOICE OF ACTION IS TO DEDICATE OUR LIVES TO HIS DYING COMMAND!!!
WE SERVED OUR MASTER ODEN! WE WERE MEANT TO BE HIS SHIELD!!
AND IN THE END, IT WAS HE WHO SAVED OUR LIVES!!!
?!!
...AND OPEN THE CLOSED BORDERS OF OUR COUNTRY !!!
WE MUST STRIKE DOWN THE SHOGUN OF WANO...

WANO IS ESSENTIALLY IN A LOCKDOWN STATE THROUGH THE COMBINED STRENGTH OF THE SHOGUN AND KAIDO!!
THAT IS OUR DEEPEST DESIRE !!!

...BUT THEY ARE STILL MERE CHAFF BEFORE THE MIGHT OF THE ENEMY'S ARMY! VICTORY IS BUT A DISTANT HOPE.
BACK HOME, THE SEEDS OF REBELLION ARE SLOWLY BEING FOMENTED...

MY WORD...

YES. THE KOZUKI CLAN AND THE MINKS HAVE BEEN ALIGNED FOR AGES...
...AND SWORE A PACT TO JOIN OUR FATES AS ONE!!

OUR FIRST DESTINATION WAS ZOU!!
THEREFORE...WE WENT OUT TO SEA IN SEARCH OF STOUT ALLIES TO ASSIST OUR CAUSE!!
AND YET WE MUST WIN!!!

...ALL OF OUR WARRIORS WERE PREPARED FOR OUR INEVITABLE FIGHT!!!
AND ABOVE ALL ELSE, ME AND DOG ARE LORD ODEN'S DIRECT VASSALS!! THE DAY RAIZO ARRIVED...
DON'T SAY THAT! IT WAS ONLY BECAUSE THE ENEMY USED THAT DIRTY WEAPON AGAINST YA!!
...WE RAN INTO JUST A SINGLE TROOP OF KAIDO'S...
...AND ENDED UP IN THIS SORRY STATE AGAINST JACK'S FORCES!!
HOWEVER ...
...ONCE THE BATTLE BEGAN...
AND THUS I HAVE A REQUEST OF YOU, SIR LUFFY!!
...
?!
HEH HEH... BUT IT WON'T GO LIKE THAT NEXT TIME!! WE SHALL NOT FALL INTO THAT TRAP AGAIN!!!
RIGHT ♪...
THERE'S NO SUCH THING AS BEING DISQUALIFIED FOR FIGHTING DIRTY IN WAR...
FOR WE HAVE AN ACE UP OUR OWN SLEEVE TO UNVEIL! THE NEXT TIME WE FIGHT, THEY SHALL SEE THE TRUE POWER OF THE MINKS!!!

IF YOU ARE WILLING TO ACCOMPANY US IN OUR STRUGGLE...
IT PAINS ME TO BEG FAVORS AFTER YOU HAVE ALREADY SAVED OUR LIVES...
...BUT YOUR STRENGTH OVERWHELMS ME EVERY TIME!!
!
AND OF YOU, SIR LAW!!
...THE SHOGUN OF WANO AND KAIDO, EMPEROR OF THE SEA!!!
!
...THEN I ASK FOR YOUR HELP IN THE BATTLE TO STRIKE DOWN...
DA-DO-OM!!
THE SAMURAI AND THE MINKS!! THAT'S A LOT OF POWER TO HAVE AT OUR SIDE!!
WHOAAAA!! YEAH!! NOW THIS IS MORE LIKE IT!!!

WHAT'S WRONG WITH YOU?! ARE YOU INSANE?!!
GYA
HANG ON, DON'T COUNT THAT ANSWER!! I'LL GET HIM TALKING SENSE!!!
DON'T TURN THEM DOWN!!!
NO !!!
!!!
NO, NO, NO, DON'T YOU DARE!!!
CHA-LUNG
WE NEED TO NEGOTIATE THIS.
HUH? NAMI?!!
WHUSH
ACTUALLY, LUFFY HAS A POINT.
AREN'T YOU THE COMMANDER OVER ALL OF THESE MIGHTY MEN?!!
SPEAK UP FOR YOURSELF!! AREN'T YOU THE GUY IN CHARGE?!!
!!!
?!
WHAT ARE YOU, MOMO, JUST A FIGURE-HEAD?!!

STOP GETTING MAD AT AN EIGHT-YEAR-OLD CHILD!!!
KNOCK IT OFF, LUFFY!!
THWUD!!
SMACK!!
BAP!!
WHAP!!
WHAP!!
...!!
HIK!!
AND YOU'RE JUST GONNA STAND THERE AND CRY?!!
...!!
BUT I MUST QUIBBLE WITH YOUR METHODS HERE!!!
THAT'S RIGHT.♡ COME HERE, MOMO. I'M SORRY ABOUT WHAT OUR IDIOT SAID TO YOU.
TEK
TEK
...THAT HE DOESN'T NEED TO BE IN CHARGE UNTIL HE HAS COME OF AGE.
LUFFY, BEING AN HEIR MEANS...
LET THE ADULTS AROUND HIM OFFER GUIDANCE AND...
... MOMONO-SUKE!!
THAT IS THE WORLD...
!
ZMF...!!
...!!
HIC...
HIC
GAZE OUT UPON IT!!
RUB
RUB
SNIFF
HIC
TEK
HMM ?
TEK..

MOTHER !!
LIGHT THE FIRES!!!
WE ARE SURROUNDED !!!
YOUR FATHER...IS A FOOL OF A LORD.
!!!
...!!
DRIP
DRIP
EVERYONE FLEE!!
THERE IS AN ESCAPE ROUTE!!!
YOU MUST FLEE!!
!
LUFFY ...
BLUP!!
I WANT TO DEFEAT KAIDO !!!

KAIDO IS RESPONSIBLE FOR MY FATHER'S DEATH!!!
SNIFF!!
...
LORD MOMONOSUKE ...!!
TO AVENGE FATHER AND MOTHER!!!
I WANT TO BE AN ADULT!! TO GROW STRONG!!
?!!
MY MOTHER, TOO, WAS PUT TO DEATH!!
I WANT TO PROTECT ALL OF MY LOYAL SERVANTS!!!
SNURK!
SO I WANT YOU TO HELP ME FIGHT!!!
BUT...BUT I AM TOO SMALL!! I CANNOT DO IT!!
LUFFY !!!
YOUGARA HAVE GROWN OLD AND SENTIMENTAL.
THAT'S ALL...I WANTED TA HEAR!!
DRIP
SHUDDUP.

I GET IT NOW!!
!!
I AM BEG-GING YOU FOR--
BRF !!
WHAP !!
?!!
SEE FOR YOURSELF !!
FL
OP!
I'LL TAKE DOWN KAIDO !!!
LET'S TEAM UP!! IT'S AN ALLIANCE!!
!!
NO!! YOU'RE SUPPOSED TO GRAB IT!! LIKE BAM!!
SQUEEZ--
I AM UNWORTHY OF SUCH HELP!!
I AM UNWORTHY !!
?
AH—H!!
...

...BUT PERHAPS THE PERSON WHO GIVES LORD MOMONOSUKE THE MOST RESPECT...
...IS NONE OTHER THAN SIR LUFFY HIMSELF...
YES, HE MIGHT BUTT HEADS WITH AN EIGHT-YEAR-OLD CHILD...
HUH? YOU DON'T MIND, RIGHT?
I DON'T, BUT STILL!!
AND WHAT ABOUT OUR PACT, STRAW HAT?
AND THUS THE PACT IS FORMED.
IT'S THE NINJA-PIRATE-MINK-SAMURAI ALLIANCE!!!
WE'RE ALL ON THE SAME PAGE TO BEAT UP KAIDO!!
ALL RIGHT, THAT SETTLES IT!!
RAAAAAAAH!!
BAM!!
THAT'S SO LONG!!
DO WE NEED THE "NINJA" PART?
YES, OBVIOUSLY !!!
DO—ON!!

WRONG !!
...MEANS WE'RE FRIENDS !!!
LISTEN UP!! DON'T EVER BOW YOUR HEADS TO ME AGAIN!! DON'T GET DOWN ON THE GROUND!! AN ALLIANCE TOGETHER...
AHH, THE SANJI SITUATION !!
WE'RE MISSING ONE OF OUR MEMBERS.
WAIT, SHOULDN'T THAT HAVE BEEN MENTIONED BEFOREHAND?!
AHA.
HMM ?
NOW THAT WE'RE IN AN ALLIANCE, THERE ARE CONDITIONS!!
...SO HOLD OFF ON FIGHTING UNTIL THEN! THE GOOD NEWS IS THAT SANJI'S REAL TOUGH!
I'M GOING TO BRING HIM BACK...
HAVING HIM ON BOARD IS LIKE HAVING THE STRENGTH OF A THOUSAND!!
IT HAPPENED WHILE YOUGARA WERE ASLEEP.
I DIDN'T HEAR ABOUT THIS!!
WHAT?! BY BIG MOM?!

LION... VIPER?
SURE YOU ARE.
IN THAT CASE, I'M WORTH... TWO THOUSAND.
BAP
BAP
YEAH, IT'LL BE FINE! I'M NOT GOING TO FIGHT HER!!
I'M TAKING LION VIPER.
BUT...ARE YOU SURE?! THIS IS BIG MOM OF THE FOUR EMPERORS!!
I SEE... THAT IS GOOD TO HEAR.
GUARDIANS' DWELLING
TODAY HAS BEEN...
...A DAY OF MIRACLES !!
RAHH
RAHH
WHAT COULD HAVE HAPPENED BETWEEN THEM?
SUCH ANIMOSITY THAT EVEN A SHARED GLANCE CAUSED A FIGHT TO THE DEATH.
...THEY WERE ALREADY LOCKED IN STRUGGLE.
CHATTER
CHATTER
PEDRO AND I WERE BUT CHILDREN AT THE TIME.
I WASN'T EVEN BORN YET.
TRUE... DUKE DOGSTORM AND BOSS CAT VIPER WERE ONCE THE CLOSEST OF FRIENDS...
...AND ON THE DAY THEY FINALLY RETURNED FROM THAT LONG JOURNEY, CLOSE TO DEATH...

WE CAN WAKE UP AND GO TO SLEEP WHENEVER WE LIKE NOW!!
A FEAST OF RECONCILIATION FOR OUR TWO KINGS!!
RAAAAAAAH
ARE THE STRAW HATS HERE YET?
DO OO... OW!!
WE HAVE VISUAL CONFIRMATION...
... MASTER JACK!!!
GRRRG
TO THINK I'D HAVE TO COME BACK HERE!!
YEAH, I CAN SEE THAT...

THE MINKS ARE A VERY HARDY PEOPLE!! WHAT IF SOME ESCAPED THE GAS...
...AND THEN NURSED THEIR FELLOWS BACK TO HEALTH?
...WITH THE WORDS "RAIZO WAS NOT THERE."
I DID NOT EXPECT YOU TO RETURN TO ME...
SHEEPS-HEAD...
...!!
EITHER WAY, THEY'RE WEAKENED. IF WE INVADE, WE CAN WIPE THEM OUT IN...
MERCY ONLY BREEDS ANNOYING VENGEANCE.
IF YOU HAVE THEM ON THE ROPES, FINISH THEM OFF FOR GOOD!!
WE CANNOT TELL MASTER JACK THAT WE WERE DRIVEN OUT BY SOMEONE.
WE'LL KILL THE ELEPHANT !!!
HUH ?!!
OH!!
?!
GRRG
NO NEED TO INVADE THEM...

(Can☆, Aomori)

Q: Hey, I just noticed something!! Is it possible that in the scene where the Cat Viper is singing in the bath, he's actually singing Beethoven's Ninth? Meow-meow-meow meowww, meow-meow-meow meowww!♪

--Samurai Ryota

A: Ooh, good call! It fits perfectly. I never realized that Beethoven's Ninth had lyrics! Try singing them in music class at school.

Q: There certainly are a lot of old men in *One Piece*. Is it a consequence of the story setting that there are so many old characters? Or do you just have a bad case of "Gotta-Draw-Old-Men-or-I'll-Die-itis"?

--Bootylicia

A: I love old dudes! I think that both men and women grow deeper and more interesting as they age. They're very often fascinating figures! However, reality means that you also grow physically weaker as you age. I've always had a deep disgust for young people who insult and disrespect their elders for this inevitable fact of life. So one of the fantasies that I depict in One Piece is a world in which old dudes, old ladies, gram-grams and pop-pops are still kickin' butt and takin' names. You'll be old like them one day too. Wouldn't it be cool to be this tough?

Q: Since you're the author of *One Piece,* have you ever worn a one piece dress? Also, how old is Silvers Rayleigh?

--Jabras Rayleigh

A: I always wear a one piece while at work. Rayleigh is 78 years old. On that note, Roger would be 77, Garp is 78, Sengoku is 79, and Otsuru is 76.

Chapter 820: CATS AND DOGS HAVE A HISTORY

DECKS OF THE WORLD, 500-MILLION-MAN ARC,
VOL. 13: "BIRDIE KINGDOM"

NO WONDER THAT STRAW HAT LOOKED FAMILIAR!!
AH, I SEE!
CAT AND I RODE ON ROGER'S SHIP FOR A TIME.
YOU GUYS ALL KNOW SHANKS?!
THAT'S WHAT DOGSTORM SAID TOO!!
?!
THAT WOULD BE ONE WAY OF PUTTING IT...
WHAAAT?! YOU WERE PART OF THE PIRATE KING'S CREW TOO?!

WE ACCOMPANIED LORD ODEN AS HIS RETAINERS, EVERYWHERE HE WENT.
SO WE ALSO RODE ON WHITEBEARD'S MOBY DICK FOR A TIME.
IT WAS FROM THERE THAT ROGER SCOUTED LORD ODEN, AND WE JOINED HIM, OF COURSE.
HUH?
WAIT, WAIT, WAIT!! WHITEBEARD?!!
IN GENERATIONAL TERMS, LORD ODEN WAS MORE OF A KID OR AN APPRENTICE BACK THEN, LIKE SHANKS AND BUGGY.
WAIT, STOP, STOP!
MY MIND CAN'T WRAP ITSELF AROUND THESE FACTS!!
BUT WE DIDN'T JOIN 'EM ON THE TRIP TA RAFTEL.
OKAY, SO... ODEN, DOG AND CAT WERE ON WHITEBEARD'S SHIP, THEN...
...!!!
...?!
AHH, IF THIS AIN'T A TRIP DOWN MEMORY LANE!
WE HAD A LOT OF FUN BACK IN THOSE DAYS!!!

HOW MY HEART RACED EACH AND EVERY DAY!! HOW I MISS THOSE DAYS OF ADVENTURE!!!
AN ISLAND UNDER THE SEA!! WITH ITS OWN SUNLIGHT!!
A SEA OF CLOUDS, FLOATIN' IN THE SKY!!
WE ENCOUNTERED SO MANY UNKNOWN RACES! LANDS! CLIMATES!!
YOOK
YOOK!!
MEOW
MEOW
YOU GUYS WERE TRYING TO KILL EACH OTHER MINUTES AGO, RIGHT?
IN FACT, OUR JOB WAS TO ATTEMPT IN VAIN TO KEEP LORD ODEN FROM BOARDING THE SHIP OF A PIRATE!!
NO, WE WERE ALWAYS ON WANO!!
SO WERE KIN'EMON AND THE REST OF YOU ON WHITEBEARD'S BOAT TOO?!
CHATTER
CHATTER
FOR IN THE ISOLATIONIST LAND OF WANO...
AND LORD ODEN WAS SOMEWHAT OF A MALCONTENT...
...WHO LONG EXPRESSED DOUBTS OVER THE LAWS THAT KEPT OUR NATION CLOSED!!!
...IT IS A CRIME EVEN TO SET SAIL!!!

THEY WERE HONORABLE MEN, NOT WICKED...YET IT WOULD BE A TREMENDOUS SCANDAL FOR A DAIMYO TO RIDE WITH PIRATES.
...
AS HIS SERVANTS, OUR DUTY WAS CLEAR.
WE HAD PERSONAL CONTACT WITH WHITEBEARD, ROGER AND THEIR CREWS WHEN THEY LANDED ON WANO.
IT WAS TOM'S FAMOUS ORO JACKSON!!!
IF YOU RODE ON ROGER'S SHIP...THEN THAT WAS FROM MY SHIPBUILDING MASTER!!
!!
BO
OM!!
WHAT?! AN APPRENTICE OF TOM THE SHIPWRIGHT ?!!
RAYLEIGH TOO?!
WELL, ANYWAYS, YOU ALL KNOW SHANKS!!
YES, OF COURSE.
I'M STARTING TO WORRY ABOUT THE PATH OF OUR TRAVELS.
HMM?
SORRY TO INTERRUPT, BUT I JUST WANT TO MAKE SURE OF SOMETHING!!
WAIT, BROOK!!
THEN YOU MUST ALSO KNOW THEIR DOCTOR, CRO--
!

LOOK!
HERE'S OUR LOG POSE!!
BUT WE'RE NOT FOLLOWING IT NOW... ISN'T THAT A PROBLEM?
Om
...WE CAME HERE TO ZOU BY COINCIDENCE-- THROUGH A VIVRE CARD!
AFTER WE MET TRAFFY...
AND ALSO BY COINCIDENCE, WE GAINED THIS INFORMATION...
...ABOUT THE ROAD PONEGLIFFS !!
BUT ACCORDING TO CROCUS BACK AT TWIN CAPE...
RED LINE
...IF YOU JUST FOLLOW THE LOG, ALL OF THE ROUTES EVENTUALLY CONVERGE INTO ONE.
I JUST ASSUMED... THAT WAS WHERE RAFTEL WOULD BE...
CROCUS! WHAT A FOND, FAMILIAR NAME!
HOW IS CROCUS? IS HE WELL?!

WHAAAT ?!!
THAT WAS MY CREW, AND THEY'RE ALL DEAD NOW!!
BACK THEN, HE WAS ALWAYS SEARCHIN' FOR THIS ONE PIRATE CREW.
THAT WAS TWO YEARS AGO THOUGH!!
YEAH, HE WAS DOING GREAT!!
ARE YOU LISTENING TO ME?!!

HOWEVER, ON YOURGARA TRAVELS...
YES, I UNDERSTAND YOUR POINT. IF YOU ARE CURIOUS TO SEE WHERE THE LOG LEADS YOU, YOU ARE FREE TO FOLLOW IT...
...YOU HAVE ALREADY BEGUN THE NEXT ADVENTURE.
THERE IS A POINT WHERE ALL THREE NEEDLES POINT YOU TO THE SAME LOCATION!!

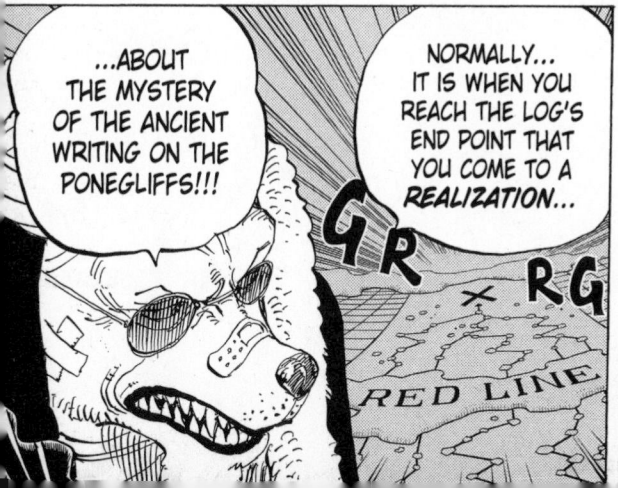
...ABOUT THE MYSTERY OF THE ANCIENT WRITING ON THE PONEGLIFFS!!!
NORMALLY... IT IS WHEN YOU REACH THE LOG'S END POINT THAT YOU COME TO A *REALIZATION*...
GR
RG
RED LINE

WHAT DO YOU MEAN?!
HUH?

...AND THE EXISTENCE OF RAFTEL, THE FINAL, UNSEEN ISLAND!!
AND THE CIVILIZATION THAT GAVE BIRTH TO THEM...
FROM THAT POINT, ROGER STARTED HIS ADVENTURE ANEW.
!
...
HE WOULD NOT LIE ABOUT THAT UNLESS HE DISLIKED YOUGARA.
CROCUS WAS A CREWMATE OF THE KING OF THE PIRATES--ONE OF THOSE WHO KNOWS ALL.
CONTINUE ON YOUR WAY!!!
DON'T WORRY. YOU ARE NOT ON THE WRONG PATH.
WHEW
OKAY!!
!!
THERE'S A FIRM HEAD ON THOSE SHOULDERS!!
ARE YOUGARA THE NAVIGATOR?

THREE CHEERS FOR THE FUTURE NAVIGATOR OF THE KING OF PIRATES!!
H-HE SAID I HAVE A GOOD HEAD ON MY SHOULDERS.♡ I MEAN, I KNEW THAT, BUT...
WHOA, THERE! I DIDN'T FOLLOW ALL OF THAT, BUT IT SOUNDS LIKE OUR NAVIGATOR'S PRETTY SPECIAL!!
HURRAH
HURRAH
WHAP
WHAP
WHAP
BWA-HA HA HA HA
YOUGARA REALLY SEEM TA ENJOY YOURSELVES.

I MET ROGER'S CREW AS WELL, BUT MY MEMORY OF IT IS HAZY.
...THAT THIS IS MAKING MY HEAD SPIN LIKE WHEN WE MET RAYLEIGH.
GOSH, YOU GUYS HAVE SO MANY CONNECTIONS TO TRUE LEGENDS...
STOP WHAPPING ME! THAT HURTS!!
GYAAA

...WERE SO RICH AND NUMEROUS, WE'LL HAFTA GO MORE IN DEPTH SOMEDAY!!
MROW-ROW-ROW! LORD ODEN'S ADVENTURES...

ROGER DIED OVER TWENTY YEARS AGO!! WHO ARE YOU GETTING HIM CONFUSED WITH?!
AH, THAT'S TOO BAD-- LIAR!!
I WAS TOO YOUNG.

WE MUST MAKE PREPARA-TIONS!!!
...BEFORE WE FIGHT KAIDO!!!
SO...THERE ARE MANY THINGS FOR US TO TAKE CARE OF...
AND BEFORE THEN, WE WANNA GET IN TOUCH WITH SOMEONE!
IT NEVER HURTS TO HAVE MORE POWER ON YER SIDE.
WHO'S THAT?
AS I EXPLAINED EARLIER, EVEN BACK IN WANO...
...WE ARE RECRUITING SAMURAI WHO WILL FIGHT FOR OUR CAUSE!!
MARCO THE PHOENIX !!!
?!!
THE FORMER COMMANDER OF THE WHITEBEARD PIRATES' FIRST DIVISION...

OH, RIGHT!! YOU GUYS ARE FRIENDS!! WILL THEY COME HELP US?!
NO, WAIT! THERE WAS THAT INCIDENT A YEAR BACK--
MARCO ?!!
DO OM!!
HIM!!!
THE ONE LIKE A PINE-APPLE.
YO!!
I'M PRETTY SURE I KNOW THAT GUY. MARCO, MARCO...
EVEN IF WE FIND HIM, THE LIKELIHOOD IS LOW.
DON'T GET YOUR HOPES UP.
...IN WHAT THE WORLD CALLS THE GRUDGE WAR!!
AFTER THAT, THE COMMANDER AND HIS FOLKS JUST UP AN' DISAPPEARED.
MARCO AND THE OTHER REMNANTS OF THE WHITEBEARD PIRATES...
...CLASHED WITH TEECH AND HIS BLACKBEARD PIRATES ONE YEAR AGO...
?!!

WHOA, WHOA, WHOA! THEY FOUGHT WITH BLACKBEARD?!
...THEN I GOT AN IDEA OF WHERE HE MIGHT BE NOW!!
BUT IF MARCO IS STILL ALIVE...
IT WAS ONLY AFTER THIS MAJOR CONFRONTATION THAT BLACKBEARD WAS FIRST INCLUDED...
...AMONG THE LIST OF THE FOUR EMPERORS!!
THEY DID... IT WAS QUITE A LARGE BATTLE, WITH EACH SIDE BRINGING IN PLENTY OF HELP.
IN THE END, MARCO'S GROUP WAS OBLITERATED.
?!!
...I FOUND OUT THAT THE WHITEBEARD PIRATES HELPED SAVE MY LIFE.
AFTER I BLACKED OUT DURING THE PARAMOUNT WAR...
TAKE ACE'S BROTHER AND GO, JIMBE!!!
IT WAS A HUGE DEAL, MAN!
SO THAT'S THE STORY!! DAMN THAT BLACKBEARD !!!

OH, OKAY! I GET IT.
WELL, MY POINT IS THAT WE STILL NEED TIME TA MAKE OUR OWN PREPARATIONS.

WISH I COULD SEE HIM AGAIN AND TELL HIM THANKS!!

IS IT SAFE FOR YOU TO RETURN? ISN'T THE SHOGUN AFTER YOU?
WE WILL FIND MORE COMPATRIOTS IN WANO AND FINE-TUNE OUR PLANS!!
THEN LET'S AGREE ON A PLACE TO MEET UP AGAIN AFTER WE SPLIT!!
YES, BUT I AM WORRIED FOR MY COMPANIONS.
I H

THERE THEY ARE!! IT'S RAIZO!!
?!!
ZZSH-!!
RAAAH

WE'LL MEET UP IN WANO--LET'S MAKE A VIVRE CARD FROM KIN'EMON.
I'LL TAKE SOME FIGHTERS AND GO LOOKIN' FOR MARCO.
AYE.

YOU'LL BE SAFE ON THE TRIP WITH OUR SUBMARINE... ALL YOU NEED IS A PLACE TO HIDE ON THE ISLAND.

WE'RE SORRY FOR TYING YOU UP, RAIZO!!
THOSE ROPES DID NOT HURT YOUR WRISTS, I HOPE!!
I'M GLAD YOU'RE WELL!!
THERE YOU ARE, RAIZO!! WELCOME BACK!!!
RAAAAAAAAHH
LET'S HAVE A FEAST!!!

AND THE SAFE REUNION OF THE KOZUKI CLAN!!!
AND THE RECONCILIATION OF OUR KINGS!!

RAA
TO RAIZO'S WELL-BEING!!!

NINPO ...
!!
GRRG...
CURSE EACH AND EVERY ONE OF YOU!!!

CURSE YOU, MINKS...

RAIZOOO !!
RAAAAAAAAAHH
I LOVE YOU JUTSUUUU !!!
POOF!
RAHH
RAHH
KYAA
NIN!! NIN!!

OR DO YOU WANT TO BE TOO LATE TO HELP SANJI?!
WE'RE GOING BACK TO THE SHIP!!
GWEH !!!
WAIT JUST A SECOND, LUFFY!! HAVEN'T YOU DONE ENOUGH FEASTING?!
RAHH
RAHH
?!
YANK!!

YEAH!! IT'S A FEAST!!!

I'M GOING TOO!! PEKOMS IS GRAVELY INJURED!! HE NEEDS A DOCTOR!!
AH.

BESIDES, HOW DO YOU EXPECT TO CROSS THE NEW WORLD SEA WITHOUT A GUIDING HAND?!
AH.

I FEEL RESPON-SIBLE.
I'M GOING WITH YOU, OF COURSE!!
HUH?! WHY WOULD YOU BE--
BURMP

I WAS THERE WHEN SANJI WAS DRAGGED AWAY TOO, REMEMBER ?!!
HEY, STOP LEAVING ME OUT OF THINGS!!
BO—NE!!
THAT WON'T BE NECES-SARY.
AH.
PLUS, WHO'S GOING TO PLAY YOU MUSIC WHEN YOU'RE FEELING DOWN?!
Ah–let's go seee the Cat Viperrrr ...
BA—m!!
THIS INFILTRATION PLAN IS GETTING LESS LIKELY BY THE MINUTE... IF YOU BUST UP THE CEREMONY, MAKE SURE TO SCAMPER BACK HERE PRONTO, OKAY?!
IN FACT, I WISH I COULD JOIN YOU! I HAVE MY OWN DEBT TO SIR SANJI... FORGIVE ME FOR NOT GOING!!
NO ONE WOULD DARE STOP YOU FROM TAKING BACK YOUR COMPANION!
I'M GONNA TAKE THEM ALONG, KIN'EMON. IS THAT OKAY?
DA-DUM
DA-DUM
RAHH
RAHH
GET SANJI BACK, GUYS!!!
ZNRR
KIAA
IAAA
RD
HUH ?
HMM ?
I'M GOING TO LOOK INTO KAIDO'S PONEGLIFF OVER IN WANO.
DA-DUM
OH, LUFFY.
IF YOU SHOULD HAPPEN ACROSS ANY PONEGLIFFS, BRING ME A RUBBING, PLEASE.
OH, SURE.
WHAT IS HE, AN ERRAND BOY?!

ZMMM!!!
WHOA !!
AAAH !!
KYAA
?!!
PAWOO
EEEK!
RAHH

ZUNESHA'S TRUMPETIN' !!
PAWOO
WHAT'S GOIN' ON?!!
THE ISLAND IS ROCKING!!!
RAAH
AAAAAH !!
EEEEK !!

RAHH
WHOSE VOICE WAS THAT?
!!
HUH ?!
KYAA

WHAT SHAKING!! THIS HAS NEVER HAPPENED BEFORE...
GRRAHHRG
KYAA

Chapter 821: UNDERSTOOD

vol.82

ONE PIECE

ZDMM
EEEK !!
RAHH
KYAA
AAAAA
AAAH !!
KRA ASH!!
AAAGH !!
GSHK GSHK
THE HOUSES ARE COLLAPSING !!
AAA
GRAB ON TO TREES FOR DEAR LIFE!!!
AHH
GET AWAY FROM THE BUILDINGS!!!

PAWOOO~!!!
LORD MOMONOSUKE!!
IT'S THE VOICE AGAIN!
RAH!
IF YOU'RE THERE...
GIAA
WHAT'S HAPPENIN' TO ZUNESHA?!!
!!
YOU TOO?!
WHAT DO YOU MEAN... YOU DON'T HEAR THAT?!
HEAR WHAT ?!!
GRRG AAAAHH
WHAT'S WRONG, LUFFY?!
IT IS THE LOUDEST VOICE I'VE HEARD YET!!!
DO IT QUICKLY !!!
WHO ARE YOUUU?!!
SHI
NG

DA DA DA DA
FIRE !!!
DOOM!!
PAWOOO ~~!!!
KADA DOOM...!!
CONCENTRATE FIRE ON THE LEFT FRONT LEG!!!
GYA HA HA HA!
EVEN AN ORDINARY ELEPHANT PANICS OVER A SINGLE BEE...
OF COURSE IT IS!!
?!
OHHH
IT'S WORKING... IT'S WORKING !!!

...THEN ITS SKIN'S GOTTA BE OLD AND DECREPIT!!
A "LIVING LEGEND"? HAH!! IT'S JUST A FEEBLE OLD GEEZER!!
DA DOOM!! DOOM!!
DA DOOM!!
IF THIS THING'S REALLY BEEN ALIVE FOR A MILLENNIUM...
AWOO
KSHUNK
KABOOM!!
THAT'S MORE THAN ENOUGH FIREPOWER.
TEAR ITS BELLY OPEN FROM THE INSIDE!!!
I CAN PLUCK OUT ITS EYES!! CUT OFF ITS TONGUE!!
...!!!
UGH!
DA DA DOOM!!
KABOOOM!!
...THEN I CAN FINISH IT OFF FOR GOOD!!!
KEEP YOUR AIM STEADY!! IF WE CAN BRING IT TO ITS KNEES AND DRAW ITS HEAD CLOSER...
RAHH
RAHH!

AWOO—!!
WABABOOM!
DOOMDOOMDOOM!!
RAAAAAH
HURRY ...
...!!
KEEEE
IF YOU ARE THERE !!!
GIVE ME THE ORDER!!
KEEEEE
?
WE DON'T HEAR ANYTHING!!
LUFFY, WHO ARE YOU TALKING TO?!
WHAT DO YOU MEAN, ORDER?!! EXPLAIN FIRST!! WHO ARE YOU?!!

I'VE HEARD THAT GOL D. ROGER AND LORD ODEN SAID THE SAME THING WHEN THEY VISITED THIS PLACE!!
I CAN'T TELL WHO OR WHERE IT IS!!!
IT'S NOT LISTENING TO ME BACK!!
BUT I CAN ONLY HEAR IT!!!
KEEEE
GRRRG..
?!!
THEY HEARD A GREAT VOICE, BUT THEY COULDN'T HAVE A CONVERSATION WITH IT!!
?!!
DO
OH!
GRURRG..
BOOM!
BA-BOOM!!
!!
KEEE

JACK IS ATTACK-ING...THE ELEPHANT !!!
WEEN
WEEN
?!!
IT'S JACK !!!
ZUNESHA'S UNDER ATTACK?!!
HOW CAN YOU TELL THAT FROM HERE?!
RRB
IN THE DIRECTION OF NINE O'CLOCK!!
WITH FIVE MIGHTY SHIPS!!
WHAT ?!
SO JACK IS ALIVE AFTER ALL?!!
THEN SEND OUT THE SHIPS!! WE MUST ATTACK JACK AT SEA!!!
YES, SIR!!!
...YOU ARE ALL IN DANGER!!
ZZRRD
IT HURTS!! IF I COLLAPSE...
MOMO!! HOW CAN YOU TELL THAT STUFF?!
IT JUST... FLOWS RIGHT INTO MY MIND!! I'M SCARED!

THE SOURCE OF THE VOICE...
...IS ZOU ITSELF !!!
?!!
ZUNESHA ?!!
DO
OW!!
A LONG TIME AGO...
LONG AGO, THE ELEPHANT COMMITTED A CRIME, AND EVER SINCE...
RAHH
RAHH
....!!
IT MUST CONTINUE FOLLOWING ITS ORDERS...
...IT HAS ONLY BEEN ALLOWED TO WALK.
THERE-FORE...
THERE-FORE...
HURP...!
KLAA
RAHH
...I JUST NEED PERMISSION THIS ONCE!!!

GIVE ME THE ORDER...
PAWOOO ...!!
KADOOM!!!
...TO FIGHT !!!

MOMO!! YOU SAY IT!!!
HUH?

IT'S GONNA FALL!! SERVES YA RIGHT!!!
GUA HA HA!! IT'S WORKIN' !!

PAWOO ...
BUT I CANNOT POSSIBLY SHOUT LOUD ENOUGH TO...
JUST YELL! THE ELEPHANT'S DYING!!
IF THE ELEPHANT GOES DOWN...
I FEEL LIKE YOUR VOICE WILL REACH IT!!
...WE'LL ALL SINK INTO THE SEA!!!

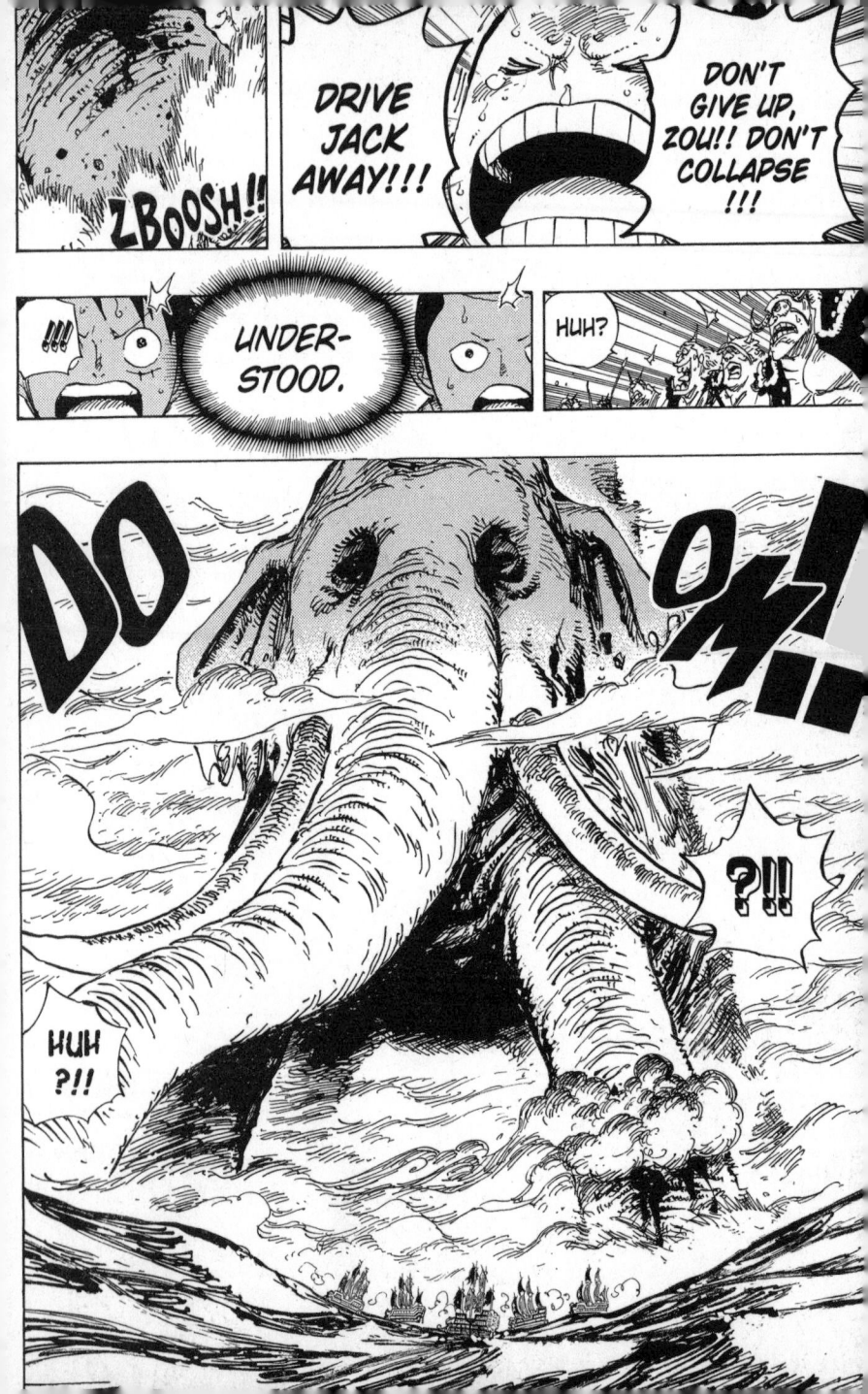
ZBOOSH!!
DRIVE JACK AWAY!!!
DON'T GIVE UP, ZOU!! DON'T COLLAPSE !!!
!!!
UNDER-STOOD.
HUH?
DO
OK!!
?!!
HUH ?!!

THE TRUNK?!!
?!!
ZZ ZSSSHH
AAAAAH !!!

BOOK

BLUB
BLUB
BLUBBLUB
PLOP
PLO-PLUP!

APE-MERGENCY !!
A...
...!!
GRRG...
GRRG...
I DON'T KNOW. I CAN'T SEE ANYTHING...
...OR HEAR ANY VOICES ANYMORE!!
WHAT HAPPENED ?!
SH
HH
IT'S CALM AGAIN!!

HUFF, HUFF...
THAT'S RIGHT!! WITH ONE BIG SWING!!
?!!
...WITH ITS TRUNK?!!
...THAT ZUNESHA SANK JACK'S FLEET...
ARE YOU SAYING...
HUR-HUR
HUR-HUR
DID LORD ODEN KNOW ABOUT THIS POWER OF LORD MOMONOSUKE'S?!
MUCH LESS THAT IT COULD COMMUNICATE WITH US...
...THAT ZUNESHA HAD A WILL OF ITS OWN!!
THIS IS TREMENDOUS. I NEVER ONCE CONSIDERED...
ZZZ
...THE BLUNT TRUTH IS THAT THIS PLACE JUST AIN'T SAFE ANYMORE!!
UNTIL WE FIGURE OUT HOW JACK GOT HERE...
WE ARE SIMPLY STUNNED BY THIS SUDDEN EVENT.
HEY, WHAT'S GOING ON?! WHY THE DARK LOOKS?!
HUR-HUR
HUR-HUR
DRAG
DRAG

SO GIVE US A WHOLE BUNCHA FOOD!!!
WELL, WE'RE ABOUT TO TAKE OFF!!
OH, I SEE. WELL, GOOD LUCK WITH THAT! HEE HEE HEE!
YOU'RE SO CARE-FREE... MROW-ROW-ROW!
WOULDN'T THAT BE CRAZY IF LOU WAS ON OUR SIDE?
ON AN ISLAND IN THE NEW WORLD
WHAT ?
CLICK!!
RRRR
RRRR!!
RRRR
OHH...
...KAIDO!!!
APPA PA PA! WE LOST OUR CONNECTION WITH JACK!
IT CUT OUT ABRUPTLY WHILE HE WAS AT SEA...

(Igarashi, Oita)

Q: I have a question for you. I'm currently in a fight with my little sister over Perona's age. Please bring an end to the hostilities. And tell us her height too. Please.

--Cherrypop, Age 12, 6th Grade

A: Perona is currently 25 years old, and she's 5'3" tall. That means she was 23 when the Straw Hats fought her. Moria took her in when she was a child, so she looks up him like a father. She believes that Moria's alive somewhere today, after his disappearance in the Paramount War.

Q: Which is more powerful, King Punch or Happiness Punch?

--Captain Nobuo

A: Well, Happiness Punch knocked out Cobra, king of Alabasta, so I doubt Elizabello stands a chance against it.

Q: The other day, this funky dude came to my house, claiming to be the missionary of a something-or-other club. He was mighty suspicious, so I called the cops on him at once, but then I wondered…was that Gambia? If so, I feel kind of bad about that.

--The Chimney Lasts Until You Get Home

A: That was a close one, actually. Gambia from the Barto Club is a missionary for the religion of "Mister-Luffyanity." He was about to give you a sermon about the miracles created by Mister Luffy and his crew of pirate disciples.

Chapter 822: DESCENDING THE ELEPHANT

DECKS OF THE WORLD, 500-MILLION-MAN ARC, VOL. 14:
"SABAODY ARCHIPELAGO--ANGRY MANAGEMENT"

A MIX OF THE MEDICAL KNOWLEDGE OF CHERRY BLOSSOM KINGDOM AND THE HERBOLOGY OF BIRDIE KINGDOM! TREMENDOUS!!
THAT SHOULD DO IT!!
THERE !!

Y-YOU CAN'T BUTTER ME UP LIKE THAT!
IT...IT WON'T WORK ON ME, YOU JERK!♡
HEH HEH HEH.♡
BRILLIANTLY DONE, DR. CHOPPER!!
RAAAAAAAAH!!
HEH HEH... ONLY BECAUSE THE FOREST HAD THE PERFECT PLANTS FOR THE JOB!!
YOU'VE TOTALLY STAUNCHED THE BLEEDING.

YEAH!! WE'VE GOT THIS!!!
WE WILL BE RESPONSIBLE FOR THAT!
YACK
YACK
BUT IT'S GOING TO BE QUITE AN ORDEAL TO CHANGE OUT THE BANDAGES.
GR RG G...

A FACT WITH WHICH WE ARE CONFRONTED ANEW TODAY.
!
...SO PERHAPS WE HAVE FORGOTTEN SOMETHING IMPORTANT.
WE HAVE ENJOYED ITS COMFORTABLE SAFETY FROM THE DAY WE WERE BORN...
...FOR A THOUSAND YEARS!!
ZUNESHA HAS BEEN OUR HOME-LAND...
GRRG...
...WHAT HAVE YOU...
RRG
...BEEN WALKING TOWARD ?!!
FOR THESE THOUSAND YEARS...
...
...BY THIS GREAT BEING BELOW US.
THAT WE HAVE ALWAYS BEEN GIVEN LIFE AND SUPPORT...
GR
R
GG...
IF IT DOES HAVE A WILL... THEN I WISH TO ASK IT A QUESTION!
AND THAT EVERY LIFE MUST EVENTUALLY COME TO AN END.
?!

HERE ON ZOU, YOU MEAN?
YOU WILL REMAIN?
KURAU CITY, MOKOMO DUKEDOM
YACK
YACK
YES.
CHATTER
CHATTER
...I WISH TO HAVE A CONVERSATION!!
IF IT IS INDEED POSSIBLE ...
I DO NOT KNOW WHAT I OUGHT TO DO! HOWEVER..
AND WHY WOULD YOU REMAIN HERE?
GROH
WHY WAS MY VOICE ABLE TO REACH IT?
DOES IT KNOW SOMETHING ABOUT THE KOZUKI CLAN?!
WITH ZUNESHA !!
THE BEING THAT HAS LIVED FOR A MILLENNIUM!!

I PLAN TO REMAIN HERE FOR A TIME.
I WILL BRING HIM WITH ME LATER!!
I HAVE BEEN THINKING THAT IT IS NECESSARY TO PROTECT ZOU FROM KAIDO'S THREAT.
IT IS FINE, KIN'EMON.
I SEE... AND YET, THERE ARE THOSE WHO AWAIT US IN WANO...
CHATTER
CHATTER
IN EITHER CASE, WE CANNOT SIMPLY ROLL INTO WANO ALL AT ONCE.
Marco Search
Team Cat Viper
Whole Cake Island
Wano
Team Luffy
Team Kin'emon
Team Zou
Dogstorm
AHH, THANK YOU!! SO WE WILL SPLIT INTO FOUR PARTIES THEN!!
YOU WANT ME TO MAKE YOU SOME? IT'S REAL EASY.
REALLY? I SAW SOME WILD ONES IN THE FOREST.
HUH ?
THE TRANSPONDER SNAILS, YOU MEAN...
I KNOW THAT FOREIGN LANDS HAVE THOSE MOLLUSKS...
THE PROBLEM IS HOW TO COMMUNI-CATE.
BUT OUR LAND HAS NO SUCH CUSTOM...

AAAAAH !!!
GO——NG!!
WHALE FOREST
OUTSIDE THE GUARDIANS' DWELLING
HEEEEY!
CHATTER
CHATTER
DO——Om!!
LION VIPER'S HOUSE FELL APART!!!
YOU ALL RIGHT?! SPEAK TO ME!!!
NO WORRIES.
I'M RIGHT HERE.
BA
m!!
KSHUNK--!!

A GUY CAN'T EVEN GET SOME PEACEFUL BED REST!!!
GOOD GRIEF!
GROWR !!!
THWUP!!
...
TUG
A TURTLE ?!
I'VE GOT THE POWERS OF THE TURTLE-TURTLE FRUIT!! AND MY SHELL'S AS HARD AS DIAMONDS!!!
I CAN SEE YOU'VE FINALLY LOST ALL SIGHT OF MY ACTUAL NAME NOW. IT'S PEKOMS!!
YOU'RE... TURTLE VIPER?!
WAIT, SO...
GROWR !!
HURP
THANKS FOR THE MEDICAL CARE. I'M EVEN MORE INDEBTED TO YA!
NO REACTION TO THE DIAMONDS REMARK, EH!! GROWR!!
AH, I SEE!!
NUDGE
NUDGE
CHOPPER SAID HE'D BE RESPONSIBLE FOR HEALING YOU UP!!
KSHUNK
ZRD

WAIT JUST A HOT SECOND!!! I'M NEARLY IN CRITICAL CONDITION OVER HERE!!
I CAN'T BELIEVE THIS!!! OF ALL THE GUYS TO OWE MY LIFE TO, IT HAD TO BE YOU!!!
SO LET'S GET GOING TO BIG MOM'S PLACE!!!
WH
AA
?!!
AT
?!!
VO
Om!!

KS
HUF!!

CHATTER
CHATTER
MURMUR
MURMUR
GUARDIANS' DWELLING

PEDRO.

HMM?
BOSS !!
CHATTER
CHATTER
THP!

...THE THOUGHT OF NOT A SINGLE MINK TAKING PART IN THE MISSION...
...WOULD BE A GRAVE STAIN UPON OUR HONOR!!
SANJI IS THIS COUNTRY'S SAVIOR...AND HE WAS ABDUCTED FROM WITHIN OUR REALM!!
I KNOW THAT IT'S A SMALL TEAM, BUT ASIDE FROM PEKOMS...
NO CUTTING IN LINE, PEDRO!!
!
YES !!
...YA WANNA GO ALONG?
YOUGARA SAYIN'...
...IS A NOISY FUSSPOT LIKE YOUGARA!!!
BUTT OUT OF THIS, SHISHILIAN!! THE LAST THING THIS MISSION NEEDS...
THE DOGSTORM MUSKETEERS INTEND TO FULFILL THAT DUTY!!!
I AM NOT NOISY !!!
DA-DO-OM!!

AND WE FOUGHT AGAINST LUFFY!! REMEMBER, PEDRO?!
RODDY!!
BB!!
I...I TOO WISH TO SERVE AS DR. CHOPPER'S ASSISTANT!!
TRISTAN!!
IN THAT CASE, LET ME GO!! I HAVE BEEN WITH THEIR GROUP THE LONGEST!!
WANDA!!
JOOK
JOOK
ME TOO!!
AS DO I!!
AND I WANT TO KEEP CHEWING ON THE BONES OF BARON CORPSE!!
JOOK
JOOK
NOW YOU'RE JUST MAKING REQUESTS!! STAY OUT OF THIS, CANINES!!
AND NAMI LOVES USING MY TUMMY AS A BED!!
WHAT GOOD WILL THAT DO, PASTOR YOMO?!
PEDRO'S THE ONLY ONE CAPABLE OF KEEPING HIMGARA IN CHECK!!
AH...
PEKOMS IS WITH HIM!!
...
BUT WHY, BOSS?!
!!
BOO
BOO
I UNDERSTAND YOUR DESIRES, MY FELLOWS!! BUT LEAVE THIS ONE TA PEDRO.

YOU JUST SQUEEZE THIS?
ARE YOU LISTENING TO ME, NAMI?!!
MUR MUR
IT'S THE TOOL OF THE CENTURY, THE--
MUR MUR
BA
THAT TOOL THERE USES POP GREEN GROWTH...
...AND HAS AN AUGMENTED SURFACE, THANKS TO FRANKY'S HELP.
IT STRETCHED !!
SQUISH!
AAH !!!
WATCH OUT!!!
AAH
AAH
I IMPLEMENTED ALL OF THE WEATHERIA DEVICES...
IT'S YOUR NEW CLIMATE BATON!!
THIS TOOL CAN EXTEND AND SHRINK FREELY WITH MINIMAL USE OF FORCE.
...THAT YOU GAVE TO ME. THE ONLY THING IS...
BECAUSE YOU EXTENDED IT TOO FAR! LISTEN TO THE EXPLANATION!!
THIS IS TOO LONG, USOPP.
YOU NEED TO PRACTICE WITH IT.
MUR MUR
MUR MUR

I KNEW YOU COULD DO IT, USOPP!!
AAAH! WATCH OUT!!
KABOOM!!
KABAM!!
GAA
SPARKLE SPARKLE
SPIN SPIN
AHH
OOH, IT'S SO EASY TO HOLD AND SWING AROUND!♡
...DEPEND ON YOU?
I DON'T KNOW WHAT YOU MEANT IN SABAODY WHEN YOU SAID YOU WANTED A "MAGIC WAND," SO THAT'LL...
JUST LIKE A MAGIC WAND!!
WHO, ME? SHUCKS...
THANK YOU, USOPP!♡
HOW WONDERFUL!♡ THIS REALLY IS THE AMALGAMATION OF ALL OF WEATHERIA'S CLIMATE SCIENCE!!
IT'S THE SORCEROR'S CLIMATE BATON I'VE ALWAYS WANTED!!
WHAT HIGH-LEVEL NINJUTSU!!
DON'T TRY TO SKIP OUT ON ME!!!
ZWOO—P
MIRAGE TEMPO!!
NOW, AS FOR THE COST OF THE MATERIALS...
FLIP FLIP!

ZOU'S MAIN GATE
YACK
YACK
CHATTER
CHATTER
SO THERE'RE SIX OF US!!
GOOD TO HAVE YOU ALONG, PERO-PERO!!
IT'S PEDRO. AND I WON'T GET IN YOUR WAY.
UGH ...!!
BE CAREFUL, NAMI!!
THANKS! YOU TOO, WANDA!
DA-
DO
On!!
I AM TAGGING ALONG WITH THE GROUP AS SOMEONE...
...WHO'S KNOWN YOUGARA FOR YEARS!!
WHAT'S THAT SUPPOSED TO MEAN?! GROWR!!
GROWR !!
WH...WHY'S PEDRO COMING ALONG...?!

IT IS WHAT IT IS!!
HEY!
THE SAD THING IS, I CAN'T DENY THAT OUT OF HAND!!
...THAT HE'S PERVING OUT AND LOVING THE IDEA OF GETTING MARRIED.
LISTEN...WE KNOW HOW HE IS. THERE'S A PRETTY GOOD CHANCE...
CHATTER
CHATTER
TAKE CARE, LUFFY!!
WE SHALL AWAIT YOU IN WANO!!
SO LONG, SIR LUFFY!!
AND NOW, I SHALL ASSIST WITH THE ELEPHANT DESCENT.
I'LL HAVE THE SAMURAI OF WANO FOLLOWING MY LEAD IN NO TIME!!
I'M GONNA GET WORKIN' ON SOME ANTI-KAIDO WEAPONS!
IF ANYTHING HAPPENS, JUST CALL US!!
NO NEED, KANJURO !!

TUMP!
?!
HMM?
ZOOP!
BYE!!
DON'T WORRY-- WE'LL GET SANJI!!
!!!
WHAAA --?!!
HA HA HA

AA AAAA AAAAAHH...

AAAA AAAA AAAA

YEAH!! HERE WE GO!!!

?!!

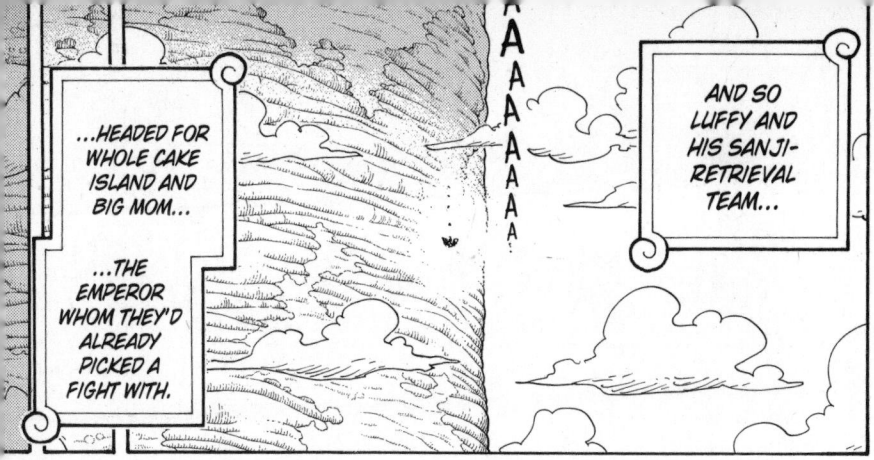
AND SO LUFFY AND HIS SANJI-RETRIEVAL TEAM...
AAAAAAA
...HEADED FOR WHOLE CAKE ISLAND AND BIG MOM...
...THE EMPEROR WHOM THEY'D ALREADY PICKED A FIGHT WITH.

MEANWHILE, ON THE GRAND LINE...
HURRY, FATHER!!
SLOW DOWN, VIVI!! WHY ARE YOU IN SUCH A GOOD MOOD?
HEE HEE!
...IN ALABASTA, THE KINGDOM OF SAND...
CHUG'TER
CHUG'TER
WHEE
WHEE

CAN YOU BLAME ME?
IT'S BEEN SO LONG...
...SINCE I WAS LAST AT SEA!!
BO
On!
QUACK ~~!!

SBS Question Corner

(Pekoms, Miyagi)

Q: Hello, Oda Sensei!! When the Straw Hats' bounty posters got updated, I was so excited! By the way...where and how did Nami's bounty picture get taken? It's so sexy… ha ha ha.

--Yutiko Loves Nami's Voice

A: It's the second time in a row she's been doing a centerfold pose. In both cases, the situation went like this:
"Hello, I'm a writer for Blah-Blah Weekly (this part is a lie)! Wow, you're gorgeous!! May I take your photograph to put on the cover of our magazine?"
"Well, if you insist. As long as you make me look good!♡"
"Click!!"

Q: Personally, everything about Nami in the New World is right up my alley. I'm all about enjoying my Nami love through anime, merchandise, figures, game DLC, and so on. As the author, do you think it's sleazy that this is one my main sources of enjoyment for the series?

--B.S.L.

A: I feel like Nami's gotten more popular lately. Maybe it's because she hasn't been around for a bit? Anyway, you're feeling guilty about thinking of the characters in a naughty manner, aren't you? (laughs) Well, I have no problems with this--for any of my characters. A teacher of mine said that your manga world is a product to be sold, and a real professional doesn't tell the customer who bought it how they should enjoy it. I agree with that philosophy. You may interpret, fantasize, and enjoy it however you wish. I'm just happy knowing that you're reading.

Q: Was Nami named for her dy*namic* breast size?

--Hiromu

A: Umm, don't parents usually name their children when they're newborns?!

Chapter 823: THE WORLD IS RESTLESS

DECKS OF THE WORLD, 500-MILLION-MAN ARC, VOL. 15:
"NOT GOING BACK TO THE BOWIN ISLANDS YET"

TAKE CARE!!
ALABASTA, KINGDOM OF SAND
MARINE
HINA
ALABASTA
RAAAAHH
SHE'S FEELING LIKE A PIRATE AGAIN, I SUPPOSE.
VIVI LOOKED VERY EXCITED TO BE OUT.
KAAA
KAHH
JUST WHEN SHE SEEMED TO BE ACTING REGAL...
PRINCESS VIVI!!
RAAAA
YOUR MAJESTY !!
PRINCESS VIVI!!
OUR EXPECTED ARRIVAL IS...
...TO MARIJOA, SAFE AND SOUND!!
I WILL BE ESCORTING THE NEFELTARI FAMILY...
?!
NAVY, HQ REAR ADMIRAL
HINA
I'VE JUST LEFT ALABASTA.
HELLO... HINA SPEAKING.
HINA
FSSH

PLEASE GET DOWN FROM THERE!!
PRIN-CESS VIVI!!!
FLAP FLAP...
FLAP.
AHH, WHAT A LOVELY SEA BREEZE!!
PRINCESS OF ALABASTA
NEFELTARI-VIVI
PRINCESS !!
COO!
SHHHH !!!
DON'T BE SUCH A WORRYWART. VIVI'S HAD EXPERIENCE AS A PIRATE--
WHAT IF A SNIPER HAS HIS WICKED SIGHTS TRAINED UPON YOU?!!
WHAT IF A METEORITE FALLS UPON YOUR HEAD?!!
WHAT IF A GREAT MONSTROUS BIRD SHOULD APPEAR AND SNATCH YOU AWAY?!!

IF YOUR HEALTH IS POOR, WE WILL PULL BACK AT ONCE.
PLEASE TAKE CARE, YOUR MAJESTY.
NO! I AM FINE...
ZUUUN...
WUEN
HAVE YOU LOST YOUR MIND, PELL?! THE NAVY IS ALL AROUND US!!
KOFF KOFF!
...I HAVE HAD QUESTIONS FOR THE WORLD GOVERNMENT...
DO
EVER SINCE THE DAY I MET NICO ROBIN...
...BETWEEN ME AND MY DREAM.
TOO MANY OBSTACLES STOOD...
OK!
KING OF ALABASTA
NEFELTARI COBRA
I AM DETERMINED TO ATTEND THIS YEAR'S REVERIE!!
EXACTLY.
ABOUT THE PONEGLIFF, YOU MEAN?

...WHAT IT WAS THE NEFELTARI KINGS OF THE DISTANT PAST DID TO THE WORLD!!
WHUP!!
...I WISH TO LEARN...
IF POSSIBLE ...
MI-MI-MI-MI-MI!♪
TMP!
THUD!!
GAKH!! KOFF!!
WATCH OUT, WATCH OUT, WATCH OUT, WATCH OUGK...
LISTEN, I'VE GOT PILES AND PILES OF PICTURES OF SUITORS!
I MIGHT NOT LAST LONG... IF ONLY MY DAUGHTER CAN FIND A HUSBAND BEFORE IT'S TOO LATE.
HMM... NOT WELL.
HOW DO YOU FEEL, FATHER?
ARRRGH!! PLEASE BEHAVE YOURSELF, PRINCESS !!!
KOFF KOFF!
BWA HA HA HA
TOSS THEM ALL OUT. HEE HEE!
THERE YOU GO AGAIN, USING YOUR SICKNESS TO TRY AND GUILT ME INTO GETTING MARRIED!
QUACK

OUR HISTORIC HOTEL WAS BUILT FOR THE SOLE PURPOSE...
YACK
YACK
CHATTER
CHATTER
CONGRATULATIONS ON YOUR ENTHRONEMENT, MAJESTY.
ROGUETOWN, EAST BLUE
IT ISN'T ISN'T BAD, ISN'T IT, DARLING?
IT ISN'T BAD...
...OF HOUSING THE NOBLES WHO COME TO ATTEND THE REVERIE EVERY FOUR YEARS!
I DO HOPE YOU ENJOY YOUR STAY.
RATHER PEDESTRIAN, REALLY.
A VIEW OF GOLD ROGER'S EXECUTION STAND IS THE BEST IT HAS TO OFFER.
QUEEN OF GOA
SALLY ISNTOINETTE
NOW BE GONE FROM MY SIGHT, TRASH.
I WILL.
!!
...KING STELLY!!
W-WELL, PLEASE DO EASE THE FATIGUE OF YOUR TRAVEL HERE...

...DUE TO AN EVENT THAT HAPPENS ONCE EVERY FOUR YEARS...
...IN THE HOLY LAND OF MARIJOA, IN THE CENTER OF THE WORLD.
THE COUNTRIES OF THE WORLD ARE IN A RESTLESS STATE...
GROOOO...
THE REVERIE.
DOOON!
...TO DISCUSS AND DEBATE THE WORLD'S MOST SERIOUS TOPICS...
...AND AGREE UPON A SHARED DIRECTION OF THE FUTURE.
...THE MONARCHS OF FIFTY NATIONS WILL COME TOGETHER...
HERE, AT THE VERY HIGHEST OF CONFERENCES...
RAAAAAH

...OF THE MOST POWERFUL OF FIGURES, THE MEETINGS ARE NOT ALWAYS ...TRANQUIL.
BUT GIVEN THE PRUDENT AND CANTANKEROUS NATURES...
IT SEEMS WE WILL MAKE THE REVERIE IN TIME.
THERE ARE SO MANY THINGS I NEED TO GET OFF MY CHEST!!!
THE WAR IS OVER NOW!!
SO DON CHINJAO...I MEAN, SAI, HAS NOT YET RETURNED.
KANO KINGDOM, WEST BLUE
CHATTER
CHATTER
HOW SHALL I DRAG YOU DOWN INTO RUIN, I WONDER?!!
OH REALLY, DALTON?! THE CHERRY BLOSSOM KINGDOM?!
MAAA HA HA HA HA!!!
EVIL BLACK DRUM KINGDOM, SOUTH BLUE
RMBL
RMBL!!
KRAK!!

I'M OFFERIN' TO BE YOUR DOCTOR ON THE TRIP!! AREN'TCHA HAPPY?
HEE HEE HEE
YOU DON'T HAVE TO LOOK SO DISPLEASED!!
WHAT DID YOU SAY?!
WHAAA
GRAND LINE
CHERRY BLOSSOM KINGDOM
I'D LOVE TO! THANK YOU, VIOLA!!
IT'S VEWY EXCITING.
IT WOULD BE AS MY ATTENDANT. WHAT DO YOU SAY?
I CAN REALLY GO?!
LAND OF PASSION, DRESSROSA
KTONK KTONK!
KTONK KTONK!
RAHH RAHH
WHAT'S WRONG WITH THAT?! GA HA HA!!
WHY DOES EVERYONE SEEM TO TREAT THIS LIKE A VACATION...?
IT'S LIKE A BIG FESTIVAL !!
YA WANNA VISIT THE HOLY LAND TOGETHER?!
I TURNED DOWN THE BATTLESHIP ESCORT!!
KING RIKU!!
KINGDOM OF PRODENCE
YACK
YACK
RAHH
RAHH

RYUGU KINGDOM, BENEATH THE RED LINE
I CANNOT! I'M SCARED!!
L...LUFFY MADE A PROMISE TO ME!!
PRINCESS OF RYUGU
SHIRAHOSHI
OH, WHAT A BOTHER ...
AND YOU WILL HAVE YOUR BROTHERS AND THE NEPTUNE ARMY TO GUARD YOU!!

...WE'VE GOT PLENTY OF SIGNATURES ALREADY!!
MMM, MAMBO!!
IF WE'RE GOING TO PETITION TO MIGRATE FISH-MAN ISLAND...
MAMBOSHI
...WE DON'T TRUST THE HUMANS!
OH DEAR...
BUT IF SHE DOESN'T COME, THAT MAKES IT SOUND AS THOUGH WE'RE SAYING...
KING OF RYUGU
NEPTUNE
WHEN WE MEET AGAIN...HE'S GOING TO TAKE ME ON A WALK IN A REAL FOREST UP ON THE SURFACE!!
YES, OF COURSE! LUFFY WILL BE ABLE TO TAKE YOU MUCH FARTHER, IF YOU WANT!!
BUT THIS TRIP IS DIRECTLY UPWARD! WE ARE ONLY SURFACING IN MARIJOA.
...OF OUR MOTHER, OTOHIME!
SO LET'S GO TOGETHER!!!
...
SHIRAHOSHI! DIDN'T YOU LEARN ANYTHING FROM THE STRAW HAT CREW?
FUKABOSHI
THIS UPCOMING MEETING IS THE GREATEST DESIRE...
FATHER, WHAT IF WE LET SHIRAHOSHI SKIP THIS ONE, MI-RE-DO?
RYUBOSHI

MEANWHILE, LUFFY'S GROUP...
A BIT... TO STAR-BOARD...
OKAAAY ...
FSHHH...
SWOOP
...LIKE THIS?
AH.
A BIT... MORE.
COME ON NOW !!!
PUT SOME SPIRIT INTO IT!! OR WE'LL SINK!!!
SHUT UP, YOU!! EVERYONE'S ALL WIPED OUT AT THE MOMENT...
...BECAUSE YOU HAD TO JUMP FROM THE TOP OF THE ELEPHANT LIKE AN IDIOT!!
THANK YOU... ONCE AGAIN I CAN SAVOR THE JOY OF BEING ALIVE...
OH, AND ALSO... I'LL GET YOU FOR THIS!!
ARRGH!!
SHIVR SHIVR...
73

SEE?! SHE'S PERFECTLY FINE...
I'VE GOT IT!!
OKAAAY !!!
BO-LO!!
CLUCK!
NOW WE'RE A BIT OFF COURSE. TURN TO PORT...
SEE ...?
WHA--!!
...FEELS LIKE IT'S FLOATING IN THE AIR!!
RABBIT
WOW!! WE REALLY ARE ON THE WATER!!
THIS BIG HEAVY BOAT...
WHAT ARE YOU DOING HERE?!!
WHAAAAAAA
MINK MUSKETEER
CARROT
BOOM!!
CARROT!! WHY?!
?
CARROT ?!!

CHOM—P!!
GARCHUUU! ♡
AAAGH !!
I DECIDED TO TAG ALONG! ♡
NO, DON'T TURN AROUND!! WANDA'S GOING TO BE FURIOUS WITH ME!!
SORRY, WE HAVE TO TAKE THE SHIP BACK.
GUZUZU
BARON CORPSE! ♡
CHOPPER! ♡
NAMIIII! ♡
OW, YOU'RE HARD!
GWEH !!
CHOMP!
CHIP!
GARCHUU—!!
EEK!
I'LL MAKE SURE NOT TO CAUSE TROUBLE! I BROUGHT LUNCH (CARROT), JUICE (CARROT), SNACKS (CARROT), EXTRA CLOTHES...
PLEASE!! I'LL DO ANYTHING! JUST TAKE ME WITH YOU!!
I ALWAYS WANTED TO GO ON AN ADVENTURE AT SEA!!
SO YOU'D RATHER BE A BOTHER TO OUR SAVIORS, CARROT?
WAA—H!!
SOB SOB...
WE ARE INFILTRATING THE LAIR OF AN EMPEROR OF THE SEA, NOT GOING OUT TO HAVE FUN!!

EVEN GOING STRAIGHT THERE?!
WHAT?! IT'LL TAKE MULTIPLE DAYS?!
HOW CAN ANY PLACE BE SO BIG?!
A GOOD HALF DAY! I MEAN, THE SEA'S A BIG PLACE, RIGHT?!
HOW LONG IS THAT GONNA LAST YA?
ZRP...!
I'VE NEVER SPENT THE NIGHT AWAY FROM HOME!♡
IT'S SEA, NOT LAND.
...IS A WONDER-LAND!!!
TRULY, THE OCEAN...
BA—...M
!!
WHO SAID YOU COULD EAT MY CARROTS?!!
CHU
MP!
AAAAGH!!!
YEAH! DON'T WORRY, I CAN...
CAN YOU FEND FOR YOURSELF IN A FIGHT?
WELL, YOU'RE ON BOARD NOW, SO WE'LL HAVE TO MAKE DO!
!!
UHOH
UHOH

RUB...
HWAA♡
HEH HEH HEH.
?!
RUB...
LUFFY, RUB HER HEAD!!
MY...MY THROAT !!!
GRRR
?!
FLAP...
FLAP...
WELL... SHE IS A GOOD FIGHTER.
WHEN DID YOU GET UP THERE, PEDRO?!
WOW !!
IT'S FINE. YOU CAN HAVE THE CARROT.♡
YOU'RE PRETTY TOUGH ...
GAHH!! THAT WAS CLOSE. I NEARLY DIED...
LUFFY NEARLY LOST...
GRIN GRIN
SLUMP!
GURK...
YOU'RE ALL USELESS! I'LL WHIP SOMETHING UP--YOU JUST WATCH THE WAVES FOR ME!
YAAAY !!
...
...
SOMEBODY COOK UP SOME FOOD!!
SH——---HH
I'M HUNGRY... LET'S EAT!!
GULP...!!
CHEW CHEW

...
NEWS PAPER
FLAP FLAP...!!
WHAT OTHER OPTION IS THERE?
THERE GOES MY ALLOWANCE !!
COO...!
FLAP
FLAP
WAIT, WAIT, WAIT!!!
AND IT'LL BE 5,000 BERRIES PER PERSON.
TEK TEK.
"LONG-RUMORED MYSTERY LOCATION...
GYAA
"... DISCOVERED AFTER DECADES.
RAHH
I'LL COOK!!
WHAAAT?!
KSHUF...
REAL BIG HEADLINE TODAY...
RAHH
GYAA
...
"...ALREADY IN UTTER RUIN!!"
Revolutionary HQ Discovered
"BALTIGO, HQ OF THE REVOLUTIONARY ARMY...
DO
OH!!

PLAYING PIRATES

Chapter 824:

vol.82

ONE PIECE

THE REVOLU-TIONARIES GOT BEATEN ?!!
DO — Om!
WHAAAT ?!!
?!!

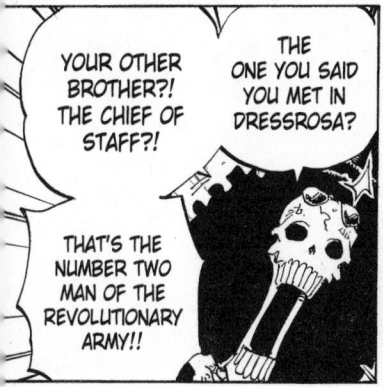
YOUR OTHER BROTHER?! THE CHIEF OF STAFF?!
THE ONE YOU SAID YOU MET IN DRESSROSA?
THAT'S THE NUMBER TWO MAN OF THE REVOLUTIONARY ARMY!!

OH! SABO!! THAT'S MY BROTHER!!
AND YOUGARA ARE...THE REVOLUTIONARY DRAGON'S...
HMM ?!!

...MONKEY D. DRAGON, THE REVOLU-TIONARY.
YOUR FATHER'S NAME IS...

LIKE... YEAH?
REMEMBER WHAT YOUR GRANDPA SAID TWO YEARS AGO!

HUH...? THEN THIS GUY "DRAGON" NEXT TO HIM IS...
WHAT KIND OF TRIO OF BROTHERS ARE YOU?!

...IS YOUR FATHER, REMEMBER ?!
...
DRAGON, CHIEF COMMANDER OF THE REVOLUTIONARY ARMY...
DA-
DO
OH!!!
YOU JUST PUT IT TOGETHER ?!!
WHAT?! LUFFY'S FATHER IS THE BOSS OF THE REVOLUTIONARIES?!
...!!
HAAA!
THAT'S MY DAD?!!
WELL, A PICTURE'S NOT THE SAME AS SEEING SOMEONE IN REAL LIFE, YO HO HO HO!
YO HO HO
HEY, LUFFY!
MORE IMPORTANTLY, I'M WORRIED ABOUT SABO!!
OHHH. IT'S THE FIRST TIME I'VE SEEN HIM! DOESN'T LOOK LIKE ME.
WHY WOULDN'T YOU BE CURIOUS?! YOUR FATHER'S SO FAMOUS!!
ROBIN SAID SHE WAS WORKING UNDER HIM ALL THAT TIME WE WERE APART!!

BUT BY THE TIME THE NAVY AND CIPHER POL ARRIVED...
...THE BLACK-BEARD PIRATES HAD ALREADY LEVELED THE SETTLEMENT TO THE GROUND.
CHOMP!
HEY! HEY, LUFFY!
IT SAYS THAT THROUGH AN ANONYMOUS SOURCE...
...THE LOCATION OF THE ARMY'S HQ WAS REVEALED!!

...ATTACK THE REVOLU-TIONARIES?!
WHY WOULD BLACKBEARD ...

BLACK-BEARD ?!!
THOSE GUYS!!!

BUT THERE WAS NO INFO ABOUT FATALITIES IN THE ARTICLE.
IT SAYS BLACK-BEARD CLASHED WITH CIPHER POL BRIEFLY BEFORE FLEEING.
UM, HEY!!

THAT CHAMPION GUY FOUGHT SABO BACK IN DRESSROSA...
MAYBE THAT HAD SOMETHING TO DO WITH IT?

GEEZ, WHAT IS IT ALREADY ?!
HEY! LUFFY!!
SO PERHAPS WE CAN ASSUME THEY'RE STILL ALIVE.
OH... YEAH! GOOD POINT!
...THAT WOULD HAVE BEEN MAJOR NEWS.
IF YOURGARA FATHER OR BROTHER WERE CAPTURED OR KILLED...

AAAH
AAAH!! I FORGOT TO TURN OFF THE STOVE!!!

FWOOOOM!!!
?!!
FIRE ?!

THANKS FOR COOKING AND EVERYTHING, BUT IS THAT SUPPOSED TO BE HAPPENING?
?

THERE'S A STORM COMING!!!
WHAAAAAT ?!!

WAIT !!
GIRRG...
?!

PUT OUT THE FIRE!!
AAAH!! SOME-THING EXPLODED !!

KABOOM!!
!!

WHEW!! THAT'S LUCKY!!
SWARK!
NOTHING ABOUT THIS IS LUCKY!!!
WHAT ABOUT THE FIRE?!!
THE RAIN WILL PUT IT OUT!!
GYAA
HOIST THE SAILS!! THE WIND WILL RIP THEM TO SHREDS!!!
RAHH
EEEEK !!!
RMBL RMBL
WHAT IS THIS?! ELECTRO ?!!
PSHA !!
KAKUETA
TAKA !!
DO-
I'M HALF-DEAD! GROWR!
YOU HELP TOO!
RMBL RMBL..!!
YAAH !!
AAGH !!
N!!!
YOU'RE SAYING...
...CARROT IS OUT AT SEA RIGHT NOW?!
YEAH...
GRRG..!!
ZOU

I APE-OLOGIZE, WANDA! MAYBE I COULD HAVE TOLD SOMEONE AND STOPPED HER...
WHY DIDN'T YOU TELL US SOONER, BARIETE?
BUT CARROT HAD ALREADY PACKED UP HER STUFF, AND...
...TO BETRAY YOU, WANDA!
B-BUT CARROT DIDN'T WANT...
WUMP
!
SHE BOUGHT YOUTEIA OFF, DIDN'T SHE?!
AHA! BE HONEST...
GACK!!
I WILL HAVE EXTRA GUARDS PUT IN PLACE.
PLEASE TAKE YOUR REST NOW, YOUR GRACE.
...
MOKOMO D
SHE'LL BE SAFE IF SHE'S WITH LUFFY'S GROUP.
NOD NOD!
...
I WAS MORE WORRIED ABOUT HER BEING MISSING.
IT'S FINE. I'M JUST GLAD WE KNOW WHERE SHE IS...

I ONLY HOPE THAT THE CARD WAS LOST WITH THE SHIPS ZUNESHA SANK...
BUT HOW DID THEY GET IT?!
I SUSPECT THAT THE ENEMY HAS A VIVRE CARD...
!
FSHHH
WE MUST BE VIGILANT...
INDEED.
DO YOU THINK THEY'LL COME BACK?
COME QUICK...
BLUB
BLUB
BLUB
...AND PULL ME OUT!!
COME QUICK...
DO
OH!!

IN A CERTAIN LAND...
JACK'S ATTEMPT TO RECAPTURE JOKER ENDED IN FAILURE...
WAHH !!
OHH...
THAT PUTS AN END TO OUR ARRANGEMENT FOR THOSE SMILE ARTIFICIAL DEVIL FRUITS!!

HE'S A CRYING DRUNK TODAY!!
WAAAH

THEN... THEN WE CAN'T MAKE...
... ANY MORE GIFTERS!! WAAAAH!!

POOR, POOR JOKER!! ALL BECAUSE YOU WERE SUCH A TERRIBLE WEAKLING...
AND BEFORE THE DREAM COULD COME TRUE...HE GOT WORKED OVER BY A BUNCH OF KIDS?!

IF YOU UNDER-ESTIMATE HIM...
BUT STRAW HAT'S THE MAN OF THE TIMES!

IF I UNDER-ESTIMATE HIM...
WANTED
?

GLUG
GLUG

WA
WAAAHH !!!
BUT WE SAID WE'D MAKE THE GREATEST CREW EVER, ENTIRELY OUT OF POWER USERS!!! WAAAAH!!!

?
!!!
WHUD !!
KRIK KRAK
DA FOOL
!!!
... THEN WHAT ?!!
AAAAGH !!!

GLUG GLUG GLUG ...!!
AH!
RATTL
RATTL
RATTL
RATTL...
YEEEEP!!!
HE TURNED INTO AN ANGRY DRUNK!!
I KNOW WHAT THEY CALL YOUR GENERATION!!
TRAFALGAR LAW!!
STRAW HAT LUFFY!!
URRP
!!
BUT YOU MUST REALIZE THAT YOU'VE MESSED WITH MY BUSINESS!!
LITTLE WHELPS PROUD OF WIPING OUT MERE WARLORDS OF THE SEA...
WHO DO YOU THINK I AM?!!

"ALL WE WERE DOING WAS PLAYING PIRATES"!!
...
KLANG
"RUN AWAY NOW WHILE YOU CAN."
...THOSE IDIOTS IN YOUR GENERATION!!
GLUG
WORO-RORO... HEY, I BET YOU CAN WARN...
GLUG
...KID !!!
...
"CAPTAIN"
...
...!!
EUSTASS
...
DO
OM!!!
WE PATCHED UP THE ROOF.
TUNKA-TONK!
TUNKA-TONK!
BRR, IT'S COLD!
VERY NICE WORK.
BACK ON THE THOUSAND SUNNY

AND WE KEPT THE FOOD SAFE, SO NOW YOU GET TO EAT MY COOKING!!
!!
BO
OM!
ALL RIGHT! THE STORM HAS PASSED!!
WE PATCHED UP THE ROOF THAT BLEW OFF!!
GUAAAAAA!!!
HURRRRL!!
OOH! THAT GOOD?!
YAAAY! FOOD! WE'RE STARVING!!
YAAA!!
THERE'S SOMETHING CLEAR... AND STICKY!!
AN ENOR-MOUS MASS OF JAM!!
IT'S FULL OF FISH BONES.
WHAT'S THIS BITTER PURPLE STUFF?!
LUFFY...RICE IS INEDIBLE UNLESS YOU COOK IT.
IT'S MY KITCHEN SINK CURRY!!
WHAT DID WE EVER DO TO YOU?
BONE
LION

DON'T FLIP THE TABLE OVER!!
THIS IS INEDIBLE !!!
SEE?! WE TOLD YOU!!!
BLEAAAH !!!
HURRRRL!!
SANJI WOULD BE MAD THAT YOU'RE WASTING WHAT IS TECHNICALLY FOOD!
YOU GUYS ARE REALLY RUDE CONSIDERING I MADE THIS FOR YOU.
CHOMP!!

OH YEAH. I SCREWED UP A BUNCH SO I USED IT ALL UP.
HUH?! ALL THAT FOOD WE LOADED... GONE!!!
CA-LU
NK..!
...!!
KCHACK!!

...THE CREW WAS AT RISK OF STARVATION.
WHAT ARE WE SUPPOSED TO DO NOW?!!
AND SO, IN JUST THE FIRST DAY OF LUFFY'S JOURNEY...
SANJI, COME AND SAVE US!!
I'M SO HUNGRY...
GYAAAAAAA
WHAT?!! A WEEK'S WORTH OF FOOD FOR ALL OF US?!!
I FIGURED YOU'D BE HUNGRY! HA HA HA.

WHOA, I THOUGHT THIS WAS SNOW, BUT...
RRR RRR
BIGMOM
RRR RRR
SEVERAL DAYS LATER
BIG MOM'S SHIP
SHIP-PY♪
SHIP-PY♪
MWOH HOH HOH, IT IS LE COTTON CANDY FLURRY!
IT MEANS WE HAVE ENTERED LE TERRITOIRE DE MAMA.
IT IS LE SIGNAL D'URGENCE !!
TARTE
THAT PHONE'S BEEN RINGING OFF THE HOOK...
RRRR..
...
PLIP
MM, SWEET.
...THAT HOUSES A PLATOON OF LE BIG MOM PIRATES! IF THIS WERE NOT MAMA'S SHIP, WE WOULD SUFFER...
IT IS A BASE MILITAIRE ...
VERY GOOD! THAT IS TARTE 28, THE 28TH TART!
DOES THE SIGNAL EXTEND TO THAT SPOT OVER THERE?
...BOOM! LE BOMBARDEMENT.
28
TARTE

HE AND I HAVE BEEN THROUGH FOR AGES.
TING!
THIS IS WHAT YOUR FATHER BEAUCOUP DESIRES!!
FOLLOW GERMA 66'S EXAMPLE AND ENTER THE BIG MOM PIRATES' OPERATION!!
DO NOT BE STUBBORN, MON AMI.
SHWUP!
EASE YOUR HOSTILITY. MAMA IS IN LE MOOD DE FÉLICITATIONS.
CHATTER
CHATTER
I'M ONLY GOING TO CLEAR ALL OF THIS UP!!
...AND THAT YOU WORKED AS LE CUISINIER ABOARD THE RESTAURANT IN THE EAST BLUE.
SHE IS AWARE, OF COURSE, THAT YOU ARE THE CAMARADE OF THE FOOLISH STRAW HAT...
IN FACT, SHE ADMIRES YOU FOR THESE QUALITÉS!!
DO

ENOUGH OF THE JOKES!!!
CLINK...
DEPENDING ON YOUR SKILL, SHE MAY OFFER YOU AN EVEN BETTER POSITION.

...IS TO COOK FOOD FOR MY COMPANIONS, NOTHING ELSE!!!
THE ONLY USE FOR THESE HANDS OF MINE...

AHH, YOU MEAN PEKOMS...
BEGE WAS RIGHT.
HE MADE HIS BUSINESS PERSONAL.

...WHO DESTROY THEIR OWN PARTNERS WITHOUT BLINKING!!
I WOULD NEVER MAKE A DISH FOR THE KIND OF PEOPLE...

I'M SURE THEY'RE MISSING MY FOOD BY NOW...
I SURVIVED A HORRIFYING HELL TO TRAIN MY SKILL!!
MWOH HOH HOH! C'EST ABSURDE!!
I CAN SEE THEIR TEARFUL FACES.

IT'S A LI'L GIFT TO YA...
WE'VE GOT A PHOTO OF LADY PUDDING FROM WHOLE CAKE ISLAND, LELO!!
VITO?
BARON TAMAGO!!
!
THE 35TH DAUGHTER OF THE CHARLOTTE FAMILY...
THIS IS YOUR BRIDE-TO-BE.
GLARE..
THAT'S NO DIFFERENT FROM SEEING HER A FEW DAYS AHEAD! I'M NOT GETTING MARRIED!!!
AFTER ALL, IT'S HARD TO MARRY A GIRL YA JUST MET...
JUST TAKE A LELO-LOOK.
...RIGHT ON THE SPOT...
BO
...
PUDDING !!
!!!
CHARLOTTE ...

SBS Question Corner

(Hiramegu, Kagoshima)

Q: Hello, Oda Sensei. Doflamingo certainly grew to a very large size. What are his favorite and least favorite foods? Does he like apples? Does he hate green peppers?

--Donuts

A: Let me guess: you like apples and hate peppers? Doflamingo's favorite food is lobster. His least favorite is barbecue. Too bad, barbecue's really tasty and fun. I guess he has some bad memories about it. Go figure!

Q: I noticed that the reindeer mink Chopper fell in love with is also on a T-shirt worn by another mink. He's a rival!

--Takataka

A: Yup, there she is on the shirt. You'll notice it says "Milky." Milky is the madonna of the Guardians!! You're correct that she's a reindeer; that's the only species of deer in which the females grow horns too. It's a chance Chopper might never get again. Think he'll make a move on her?

Vol. 81, Chapter 807

Q: Odacchi, I ask thee: why doth Sabo grow out his hair? Select any and all that applyeth. 1. To copy Ace. 2. To show off his blond hair. 3. To look cool for Koala. 4. For fashion. (Personally, the third option wouldst make me happiest.)

--Sweat Ninja

A: The answer is: 5. To hide the large scar on his face. If you look closely, you'll notice that when facing him, the part is slightly to the left, leaving more hair to fall over the right side of his face. In his case, the scar isn't exactly a badge of honor.

Chapter 825: COMIC STRIP

DECKS OF THE WORLD, 500-MILLION-MAN ARC, VOL. 16: "WEATHERIA--GOTTA DRESS TO IMPRESS FOR WHEN NAMI VISITS AGAIN"

*WORLD ECONOMIC JOURNAL

"THE NAVY IS ALWAYS JUST AND MIGHTY" AND SO ON!! NYOLOLO!!
BIGMOM
FROM WHAT I HEAR, THE STORY WAS BASED ON THE TRUE EXPLOITS OF HEROES WITHIN THE NAVY.
BUT THAT WASN'T WHAT GOT ME FASCINATED WITH IT!!
IN OTHER WORDS, IT WAS PROPAGANDA FOR THE KIDS!!
THE ARMY OF EVIL THAT USED A VARIETY OF FORCES AND WEAPONS TO PUT THE SCREWS ON SORA EACH TIME!!
CHATTER
CHATTER
IT WAS GERMA !!
AS A MATTER OF FACT, I'M EXCITED TO MEET YA IN PERSON AT LAST!
NYOLOLO! DON'T BE LIKE THAT, PAL!
DON'T INCLUDE ME IN THAT GROUP! I HAVE NOTHING TO DO WITH THEM!!
YOU GUYS WERE THE BEST, MAN!! NYOLOLOLO!
SURE, THEY ALWAYS LELO-LOST IN THE END...BUT I CHEERED LIKE HELL FOR 'EM!
MURMUR
MURMUR
TELL THEM, NOT ME.

DOO~DOOR~♪
CREAK~...
!
HEY!! OPEN UP!!
KNOCK, KNOCK!
HMM...
UMF...
ZZZZ...
THIS IS MY ROOM! DON'T FOLLOW ME IN HERE.
SO, LIKE I WAS SAYING...
WHAT, YOU HAVEN'T GIVEN UP YET?! NYOLOLO!
WE WERE ORDERED TO CAPTURE YOU AND BRING YOU BACK, CAESAR!!
I DON'T DESERVE THIS KIND OF SHABBY TREATMENT!! I'M A GENIUS SCIENTIST!!!
KS HANK!!
IT'S MY ROOM TOO!!!
SO LET ME OUT, DAMN YOU!!!

HE'S WORTH A LELO-LOT MORE!! NYOLOLO!!
I'M NOT GETTIN' MARRIED! NOW GET OUT!!
FUMP
BUT THIS GUY'S A DIFFERENT STORY!!
HE'S THE BRIDEGROOM TO TIE THE VINSMOKE AND CHARLOTTE FAMILIES TOGETHER!!
HE JUST SAID SOME-THING RUDE TO VITO!!
CH-CHK!!
GET OUT ?!!
THANKS FOR STICKING UP FOR ME, BUDDY, BUT WE'RE JUST PLAYIN' AROUND!
IT WASN'T ANYTHING THAT BAD!!
WE'RE NOT PLAYING AROUND, GOTTI. NOW YOU AND VITO GET LOST!!
WHOA, WHOA, HANG ON, GOTTI!!
FIRETANK PIRATES HIT MAN GOTTI

I'M NOT HERE TO MAKE FRIENDS...
NAH, DON'T BOTHER FORGIVING ME.
CLANK!!
THAT'S IT!! YOU'VE DONE IT!! I DON'T CARE ABOUT MYSELF, BUT I WON'T FORGIVE ANY MAN WHO INSULTS MY PALS!!
EWUCH!
TAKE IT EASY! LELO-LET HIM OFF THE HOOK!!

...THEN THE GODFATHER'S HEAD WILL FLY FROM HIS SHOULDERS!! DON'T YOU GET IT?!!
IF YOU PUT SO MUCH AS A SCRATCH ON HIS FACE...
DO
Om!

EEP!!
GOTTI!!!
GRRG
DO YOU REALIZE...THAT'S THE SON OF VINSMOKE?!

THERE'S SOMETHIN' REAL FAMILIAR ABOUT...
I SWEAR ...

NYOLOLO! SORRY, WE CAN CATCH UP ABOUT GERMA NEXT TIME!
OW OW OW! I'M SORRY, MA'AM, I'M SORRY!!
MAYBE I SHOULD JUST CUT YOU FIRST, YOU GREAT OAF!!
PLEASE DON'T.

A FEW DAYS LATER, ON THE THOUSAND SUNNY
FLASH!!!
IT'S AHH OVAH...
FZZT!
GONNA DIE...SO HOD...
FZZT!
I DEAD...
FZZT!
I'NG SHIHHUH... (I'M SHRIVELING UP.)
BO—Om!
IT'S SO VERY HOT... I THINK I MIGHT TURN INTO A MUMMY.
INDEED... WE MINKS ARE SUSCEPTIBLE TO HEAT TOO...
I CAN'T TAKE THE HEAT... I WISH I COULD REMOVE MY FUR...
HANGIII HIII... (SANJI, FOOD. ICE CREAM.)
A MUMMY...
NAMI, DO YOU SUPPOSE THAT WOULD COUNT AS A REJUVENATION FOR ME?
WHO CARES ?!
IN THAT CASE, MIGHT I HAVE A LITTLE PEEK AT YOUR PANTIES?
I DON'T EVEN HAVE THE ENERGY TO SMACK YOU...
NAMI, I'M SO HUNGRY AND HOT...
I NEED NUTRIENTS !!

I'D LOVE TO DO THAT, NAMI...
OR WE'LL ALL STARVE BEFORE WE REACH OUR DESTINATION.
WE'VE GOT TO CATCH SOME FISH BEFORE THE WEATHER CHANGES AGAIN!!
FINALLY IT'S SUNNY AGAIN!!
LACK OF FOOD, AN INABILITY TO FISH DUE TO DAYS OF STORMS...
DON'T LOOK AT ME LIKE THAT!!!
EMERGENCY... FOOD SUPPLY ...
WHAT ?!
...IT'S BOILING BENEATH US!!
BUT THE WATER'S SO HOT...
FANT...
FANT
WE WON'T GET ANY FISH THIS WAY...
BUBB
BUBB
YOU CAN DO IT!!
COME ON, LUFFY !!!
PULL, LUFFY!!
FOOD...
ARRRGH !!
YOU'VE GOT A BITE ON YOUR LINE!!
!! HR R G
LUFFY!!

SPLOOOSH!!
!!!
IT'S ENORMOUS!!
GROWR!!
LICK..
YES!
FOOOOD !!!
WAIT, LUFFY!! I'VE GOT TO LOOK UP THIS FISH FIRST!!
WHOA! IT'S A WEIRD COLOR THOUGH!! IS IT EDIBLE?!
ZWU
DD!!

LUFFYYY !!!

FOUND IT!!

SHEESH! EVERYTHING ON SANJI'S BOOKSHELF IS FULL OF NAKED PEOPLE!
FWAP
FWAP!
TOSS!
TOSS!
WHERE'S THE BOOK OF FISH?

LUFFYYY !!!
EWW, THAT PART IS SLIMY!
HERE, TRY IT OUT, CARROT!!
MMMM, THIS SKIN IS GREAT!!
WAIT, LUFFY! I'LL COOK IT!
MUNCH
MUNCH
DOO
OM!!

WATCH OUT FOR THE SKIN!! THERE'S POISON IN THAT KIND OF FISH'S SKIN!!
LOOK, SANJI EVEN INCLUDED A NOTE!!

WELL, I COOKED IT JUST THE WAY SANJI NOTED.
CHOMP CHOMP
IT'S GOOD!! IT'S SO GOOD, NAMI!!!
BAA
AM!!

CHOMP
CHOMP
MUNCH MUNCH
!!

L-LUFFY'S... GONNA DIIIE!!
S-SO... C-COLD...
HIC
SOB...
SHIVR SHIVR
YOU EAT UP TOO, CHOPPER! YOU NEED YOUR STRENGTH!!
DO——OM!!
I KNOW THAT, BUT WE CAN'T JUST SNAP OUR FINGERS AND FIND LAND...
NOM!
WE GOTTA FIND AN ISLAND SOON, NAMI!!
YUM!
CHOMP CHOMP CHOMP
I DON'T HAVE ENOUGH MEDICINE!
CHOMP CHOMP
SNIF SNIF
HIS VITALITY IS TOPS AMONG ALL OF HUMANITY.
I'M FINE... I'M JUST LOOKING...AT THE PRETTY RIVER...
LUFFY, ARE YOU GONNA DIE?
AND REMEMBER HOW THE BOOK SAID THAT THE POISON CAUSED INSTANT DEATH?!
HE'S LOOKING AT THE RIVER STYX!!!
FSHHH
WELL, LUFFY'S STILL ALIVE!! MAYBE HE HAS SOME POWERFUL RESISTANCE TO IT?

HUH? WHAT IT IS NOW, SNOW?
WAIT, NO. THOSE ARE...
SUGAR CLOUDS ?!
?!
WE'RE BOUND TO CATCH UP TO THE TERRITORY ANY MOMENT NOW...
BASED ON THE PASSAGE OF TIME, BLACK-LEG SHOULD ALREADY BE AT THE ISLAND.
TERRITORY ?
RIP RIP!!
BEE-BEE-BEEP...
TERRITORY SEA SLUGS
DID YOU SAY COTTON CANDY?!
THAT'S A COTTON CANDY FLURRY.
EXACTLY.
BLUB...
BLUBBLUB...
BEE-BEEP...
YOU ALL GOTTA HIDE OR GET INTO DISGUISE!!
IT'S JUST INTERCEPTING THE WARNING SIGNAL. WE'VE ENTERED BIG MOM'S TERRITORY.
IT'S A TRANSPONDER SNAIL! BUT FROM WHOM?
RRRRRR
COTTON CANDY!
IT'S SO SWEET!!
RRR RRR RRR !!

I'LL HANDLE THIS. YOU ALL STAY QUIET. GROWR!
THAT'LL BE OUR TARTE SCOUT SHIP!!
I HOPE THEY'VE GOT ANTIDOTES.
DAMN, ALREADY ?
I SEE SOME-THING AHEAD...
... PEKOMS.
WE IDENTIFY THIS AS THE SHIP OF THE STRAW HAT CREW.
THIS IS GERMA...
DO
OM!!
?!!
?!!
HUH ?!!
GRRG..
WHAT ?!!
NO!! THAT SHIP BELONGS TO GERMA 66!!!
BAM!!
DO
OM!!

(Hippo Iron, Saitama)

Q: I want the Cat Viper's birthday to be November 22, since it can be interpreted as "Good Meow-Meow." Is that okay?

--I Love Cats

A: Whaaaat?! Okay.

Q: Hey, Masao! The guy in the SBS of Volume 81 whose birthday was December 14!! I've come to make your dream come true!! Pica's birthday will be December 14, because it kind of sounds like "controls stone freely"! What say you, Odacchi?!

--Pitera

A: How kind! (laughs) Masao was upset that no characters shared his Birthday! Well, there you go! You have to speak in a funny high-pitched voice from now on.

Q: Heso, Oda Sensei! I was checking the birthday list and noticed that none of the Alabastan characters aside from Vivi had birthdays, so I did my best to fill them in.

King Cobra (February 13)
Bu (Ko-bu-ra) is 2, the King card is 13

Karoo (November 8)
"Ka" and "u" are 118 on a phone keypad

Pell (August 23)
Falcon is "Hayabusa," ha-bu-sa is "823"

Chaka (April 26)
Jackal, ji-ka-ru is "426"

Koza (May 26)
Ko-za is 526 on a phone keypad

Igaram (December 6)
I-ga-mu is "126"

What do you think of that?

--Hii (Age 20)

A: Whaaaaaat?! Okay.

Chapter 826: 0 AND 4

DECKS OF THE WORLD, 500-MILLION-MAN ARC, VOL. 17: "FORMER MUGGY KINGDOM--TILLING THE OLD BATTLEGROUND"

....!!!
....
GLARE
WHAT ARE YOU DOING HERE...
... STRAW HAT CREW?!
....!!
66
WE'RE GOING TO CRASH!!
FURL THE SAILS!!
DOOOM...!!

LOOKS LIKE WE'VE MISSED HIM.
SO IT SEEMS...
GIAA
KRAH
...WOULDN'T BE ESCORTED ON THIS SHIP...
MASTER SANJI...
SANJIII !!
WHAT GOOD LUCK...
YO HO HO!! OH GOOD, WE FOUND HIM ALREADY!!
HI, SANJI!!
SANJI !!
...KEEP CALLING ME SANJI?!
!!
HUH ?!
ARE THERE ANY ANTIDOTES ON THAT SHIP?!!
LUFFY'S DYING FROM EATING A POISONOUS FISH!!
HEY, SANJI!! WE'VE GOT TROUBLE!!
RATTLE
RATTLE
WHY DO YOU...
...

I DON'T BLAME YOU THOUGH.
YOU'VE GOT THE WRONG GUY!!
FWAP!!
MY NAME IS YONJI!!
THAT'S NOT SANJI, BUT YONJI?!! THEY LOOK IDENTICAL!!
HE'S EVEN GOT THE TWIRLY EYEBROWS, BUT HE'S NOT THE SAME PERSON?!!
MY CONNECTION TO THIS SANJI YOU KNOW SO WELL IS A SECRET, HOWEVER.
THAT'S OBVIOUSLY HIS BROTHER !!!
GERMA 66 (WINCH GREEN) VINSMOKE YONJI

NOTE: *SAN* MEANS "THREE" AND *YON* MEANS "FOUR" IN JAPANESE.

PLEASE!! YOU MUST HAVE ANTIDOTES ON BOARD!!
DON'T DIE, LUFFY!!
IT'S JUST SOME STUPID FISH POISON!! AREN'T YOU GOING TO BE KING OF THE PIRATES?!!
HE'S IN GREAT DANGER... LUFFY!! GET A GRIP, LUFFY!!!
KOFF !!
WE USED ALL OF OURS... AND IT'S STILL NOT ENOUGH!!
RATT
RATT
AAH!!!
IF YOU'RE REALLY PIRATES, WHY DON'T YOU TRY PLUNDERING OUR SHIP FOR THE CURE?!!
SORRY... I'M NOT INTO HELPING OTHERS.
?!!
IF YOU ARE SANJI'S BROTHER, THEN WE BEG OF YOU--PLEASE SAVE LUFFY!!!
POP!!
!
YONJI.
KCHIK!
JUST GIVE THE ORDER TO FIGHT...
HE'S NOT KIND AND GENTLE AT ALL!!
WHAT'S HIS PROBLEM?! HE LOOKS LIKE SANJI, BUT HE SURE ISN'T!!
ONLY THE PLAYBOY PART IS THE SAME!!
ARGH!!

STOP BEING SO UPTIGHT !!!
WHAM!!!
GWAH !!!
RATTL
URRGH!!!
RATTL
LUFFY !!
WHO WAS THAT?!
MASTER YONJI!!!
!!!
BOOM!!
INTRUDER !!
BZAP
WHO GOES THERE?!!
POOF!!
LUFFY !!
LUFFY !!
?!
LADY REIJU!!
AH!!
HOP!!

I'M AFRAID MY LITTLE BROTHER...
...IS A HEARTLESS, UNSYMPA-THETIC CREEP!
GOOD DAY. I'M SORRY ABOUT THIS.
WHAT BEAUTY! ♡
BROTHER?! YOU'RE HIS BIG SISTER?! MORE TWIRLY EYEBROWS!!
HOW DARE YOU EMBARRASS ME LIKE THAT!!
REIJUUU !!!
ZYLOO SK!!
!!
YOU'RE EMBARRASSING YOURSELF!!
SHUT YOUR MOUTH!!
GERMA 66 (POISON PINK)
VINSMOKE REIJU

...THAT UTILIZES SCIENCE TO FIGHT!
GERMA'S A BATTLE FORCE...
THAT'S THE POWER MAMA WANTS!!
BUP BUP BUP BUP BUP BUP
UH...
IS THAT FELLOW... FLOATING ?!
A NOBLE FAMILY...THAT CONQUERED NORTH BLUE WITH MILITARY MIGHT AGES AGO!!
BUP BUP BUP BUP BUP BUP
...!!
...OF A ROYAL DYNASTY?!
BUT PEKOMS... ISN'T "VINSMOKE" THE NAME...
I'VE BEEN ALIVE A LONG TIME... AND DEAD TOO, FOR THAT MATTER...
YOU SEEM TO KNOW A LOT ABOUT HISTORY, MR. SKELETON.
TEH-HEH
BUT IT ISN'T ALL IN THE PAST. WE'RE STILL A ROYAL LINE.
...AND THAT'S WHY WE WERE THE MODELS OF THAT COMIC STRIP.
THAT'S RIGHT. OUR NAME WAS SYNONYMOUS WITH EVIL AT ONE TIME...
BUP
!!
WHAT?!! IT'S THAT FAMOUS OF A LINE?!

HMPH !!
KNOCK IT OFF!!
IN THAT CASE, MIGHT I HAVE A PEEK AT YOUR PANTIES?
GONK!!
THUD
...BUT WE HAVE THE RIGHT TO ATTEND THE REVERIE.
WE OWN NO TERRI-TORY...
GERMA IS A NATION WITHOUT LAND.
OH...MY PARDON, MADAM!!
HSSSS...
DID HE EAT THE ARMORED STONE-FISH FROM THE BOILING SEA?
THESE SYMPTOMS ...
RATTLE
WHAT?! HOW DID YOU KNOW?!
RATTLE
?!
AND NOW...
...I THINK IT'S TIME TO DIG IN.
...IS MY FAVORITE. ♡
BECAUSE AS IT HAPPENS, THIS POISON...
?!
WHAT ?!!
HE'S QUITE A GLUTTON...♡ IT CAN KILL A GIANT ON CONTACT, NORMALLY.
THIS POISON HAS VERY PARTICULAR EFFECTS.
OH NO!! I'M A FAILURE OF A DOCTOR!! WAAAH!!
HSSSS
HE'S VERY LUCKY THOUGH.

WHAT?! WAIT A MINUTE!!
YOU'LL DIE IF YOU SUCK OUT ALL THAT POISON!!!
SMOOO
DOWN THE HATCH♡
CH!!!
?!!

THE RASHES ARE MOVING TO HER!!!
ZRRP...
NOT THAT I HAVE ANY LIPS TO DO IT WITH!!
OHHH!!! I'M SO JEALOUS!! SMOOOOCH! ♡♡

SMOOOOCH
GRRRLLP
...
WOW...
HUH?

AAAH...
FSSS...
GULP !!
FLOP...
THUMP...!!
PWUP♡
GRRG...
ZZZ
I AM POISON PINK!!
YES, OF COURSE...
?!
...?
...?
ZSH!!
DID YOU SUCK IT ALL OUT?! ARE YOU OKAY?!
WHAAAT?!! ALL OF LUFFY'S RASHES ARE GONE!!
BA M!
PLIP
THANKS FOR THE TREAT. ♡
DU OM!!

...?! WEEZ... WEEZ...!!
KOFF !!
KOFF !!
!!
BWAAA !!!
HU
RP!!
LUFFY !!!
WOWEE!

BUT THAT SKIN WAS SO GOOD!! IS THERE ANY LEFT?!
HUH?! I WAS JUST EATING THE FISH... DID I FALL ASLEEP?!
YOU'RE ALL BETTER NOW?!
?
I'M SO GLAD!!!
NO !!!
LUUUFFYYY !!!

HEE HEE.
HUH?! THANKS!!! WAIT, WHAT?
SHE SAVED YOUR LIFE, LUFFY!
YOU'RE RIGHT! WHO?
SHE'S A GIRL !!!
SANJI ?!!
HMM?

...FOR MY BROTHER UP UNTIL NOW.
THANKS FOR ALL YOU'VE DONE...
?!!

...
SO THAT'S STRAW HAT LUFFY.

TWO YEARS AGO, THERE WAS A BOUNTY POSTER RESEMBLING SANJI...
YES. WE WERE SEPARATED AT A YOUNG AGE...AND OUR FATHER HAS ALWAYS BEEN SEARCHING FOR HIM...
OHHH!! YOU'RE SANJI'S BIG SISTER?!
...SO FATHER HAD NAVY HQ IN HOT PURSUIT AFTER HIM.
IT TURNED OUT TO BE A DIFFERENT PERSON NAMED DUVAL.

WHEN THE GOVERN-MENT TOLD US...
...THAT BLACK-LEG SANJI WAS FINALLY CAPTURED ON FILM.
IT WASN'T UNTIL RECENTLY, WITH THE REVIVAL OF THE STRAW HAT CREW...
FSHHH...

OHHH, DUVAL!! YES, SANJI WAS FURIOUS ABOUT THAT.

...AND HAD DEAD OR ALIVE...
...TURNED INTO ONLY ALIVE ON THE POSTER.
WANTED
ONLY ALIVE
SANJI
177,000,000-
MAR!
...MY FATHER PERSONALLY BUMPED UP THE BOUNTY ...
I DON'T KNOW... WITH BIG MOM, PROBABLY. OR FATHER.
WE WERE SUPPOSED TO COME OUT TO MEET AND ESCORT HIM, BUT IT SEEMS WE'VE MISSED HIM.♡
WHERE IS SANJI NOW?!
SO THAT'S WHY ONLY SANJI'S POSTER SAID THAT!!
HE'S MY COMPANION !!!
BUT GIVE SANJI BACK!!
!!
BO
Om
SANJI'S SISTER!
THANKS FOR SAVING MY LIFE.
!

YOU SAVED AN ENEMY.
THERE, SEE?

...

WHY ARE YOU WITH THE STRAW HAT CREW?
YOU'RE PEKOMS FROM THE BIG MOM PIRATES, AREN'T YOU?!

BOOm!!
THAT'S TRUE!!
WHOA !!
!!

...AND IT AIN'T NONE O' YOURS!!
I'VE GOT MY OWN BUSINESS TO CONDUCT...
GROWR !!
UMF!!
...AIN'T GOT NO RELATION YET!!
ME AND YOU PEOPLE...

GOOD IDEA. WE DON'T WANNA GET IN TROUBLE...
...BY RUINING OUR BROTHER'S MARRIAGE. LET'S BOTH AGREE TO EXERCISE DISCRETION!!
DOON!!
I SUPPOSE THAT FOR NOW...
...WE'LL PRETEND WE DIDN'T SEE ANYTHING!
FOOT!
WANTED
BEST OF LUCK... ♡
SO LONG...
VERY SMART PLAN. GROWR!!
...
BLUBBLUB...
JIMBEI ...!!
DOON!!
SO WHAT'S THE PLAN?
THAT'S RIGHT.
BLUBBLUB
ABSOLUTELY CERTAIN... STRAW HAT LUFFY'S ON BOARD AND EVERYTHING.

SBS Question Corner

(Hippo Iron, Saitama)

Q: Oda Sensei, please draw the pirate captains who joined the Straw Hat Fleet as children! Please!!

--Thank You Pirates

A: Here you go.

Bartolomeo

Leo

Hajrudin

Orlumbus

Ideo

Cavendish & Farul

Sai

That's it for the SBS! There's more info about the upcoming movie at the end of the book. See you next time!!

Chapter 827:
TOTTO LAND

DECKS OF THE WORLD, 500-MILLION-MAN ARC, VOL. 18:
"KAMABAKKA QUEENDOM--MAKING PREPARATIONS"

FORGIVE ME! I WAS SO CERTAIN YOU WERE AN ENEMY SHIP. ♡
OHO, OHO, OHO. YES, I SEE.

OHHH!! DOES THIS MEAN YOU MIGHT BE CARRYING SOMETHING **SWEET** ON BOARD?
DO OM!
SO YOU'RE SAYING YOU STOLE THIS SHIP FROM PIRATES... ♡
WELL, MAMA WILL BE DELIGHTED. ♡
OF COURSE.

OHHH! HOW LOVELY. OHO HO HO HO! ♡ MOST CERTAINLY! ♡
IT'S A SURPRISE... DON'T REPORT THE SHIP TO MAMA.
WHAT A CHARMING GENTLEMAN YOU ARE, MASTER PEKOMS! ♡

AND NOT ONLY THAT...
ALL THE BRICKS...AND HOUSES...AND EVERYTHING...
AWESOME !!
LOOK, CHOPPER !!
CHECK OUT ALL THE DIFFERENT KINDS OF PEOPLE!!!
CHATTER
CHATTER
A WHOLE TOWN OF CHOCOLATE!!! IT'S LIKE A DREAM COME TRUE!!! ♡♡
...ARE MADE OF CHOCOLATE !!!
CHATTER
CHATTER
BLAB
BLAB
DO
Om!!
CHOCOLATE CLOTHES?!
CHOCOLATE BATHS?!
CHOCOLOUN-TAIN!!
A CHOCOLATE FOUNTAIN !!

HOW IS IT? DO I LOOK LIKE A PIRATE?
YOU LOOK SO LOVELY, NAMI! ♡♡♡
WOW, THIS IS CUTE!
EEEK ♡
BROO...
HMM ?
DO-
-On!
!
ZZSH—H
GO AND LOAD UP ON FOOD SUPPLIES.
SURE THING!
I'LL STEP ON YOU.
IT'LL TAKE ANOTHER DAY TO REACH WHOLE CAKE ISLAND.

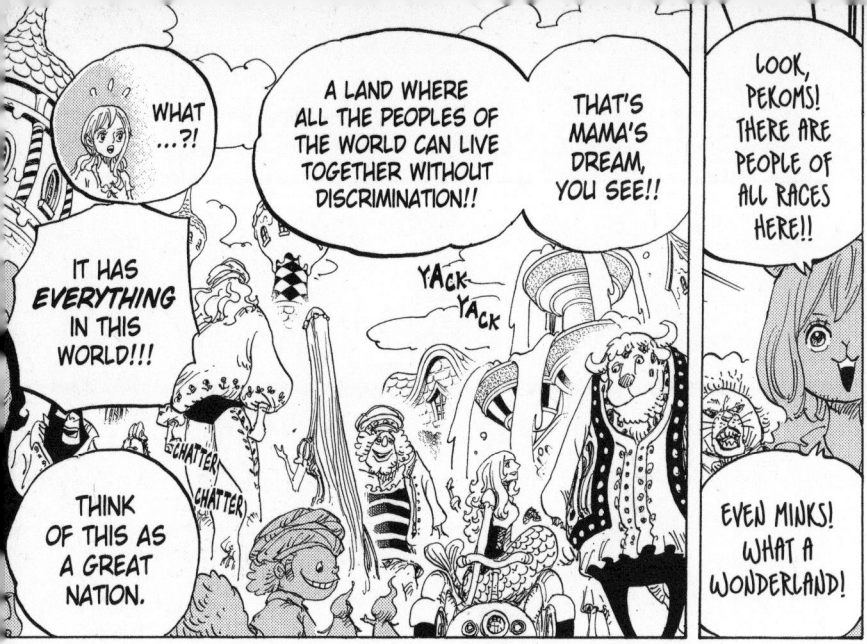
WHAT ...?!
A LAND WHERE ALL THE PEOPLES OF THE WORLD CAN LIVE TOGETHER WITHOUT DISCRIMINATION!!
THAT'S MAMA'S DREAM, YOU SEE!!
LOOK, PEKOMS! THERE ARE PEOPLE OF ALL RACES HERE!!
IT HAS EVERYTHING IN THIS WORLD!!!
YACK YACK
CHATTER CHATTER
THINK OF THIS AS A GREAT NATION.
EVEN MINKS! WHAT A WONDERLAND!

THIS ENTIRE STRETCH OF SEA IS KNOWN AS...
...TOTTO LAND, THE TOTAL OF ALL LANDS!!!
THERE ARE 34 OTHER ISLANDS SCATTERED AROUND WHOLE CAKE ISLAND...
...AND THEY ARE MANAGED BY 34 DIFFERENT MINISTERS...

...WHICH IS RUN BY THE MINISTER OF CHOCOLATE!!
BO—OM!
CHATTER CHATTER
YACK YACK
THIS HERE IS CHOCOLAT TOWN ON CACAO ISLAND...
IT LOOKS SO YUMMY! ♡
THE ENTIRE TOWN IS BUILT OF CHOCOLATE.

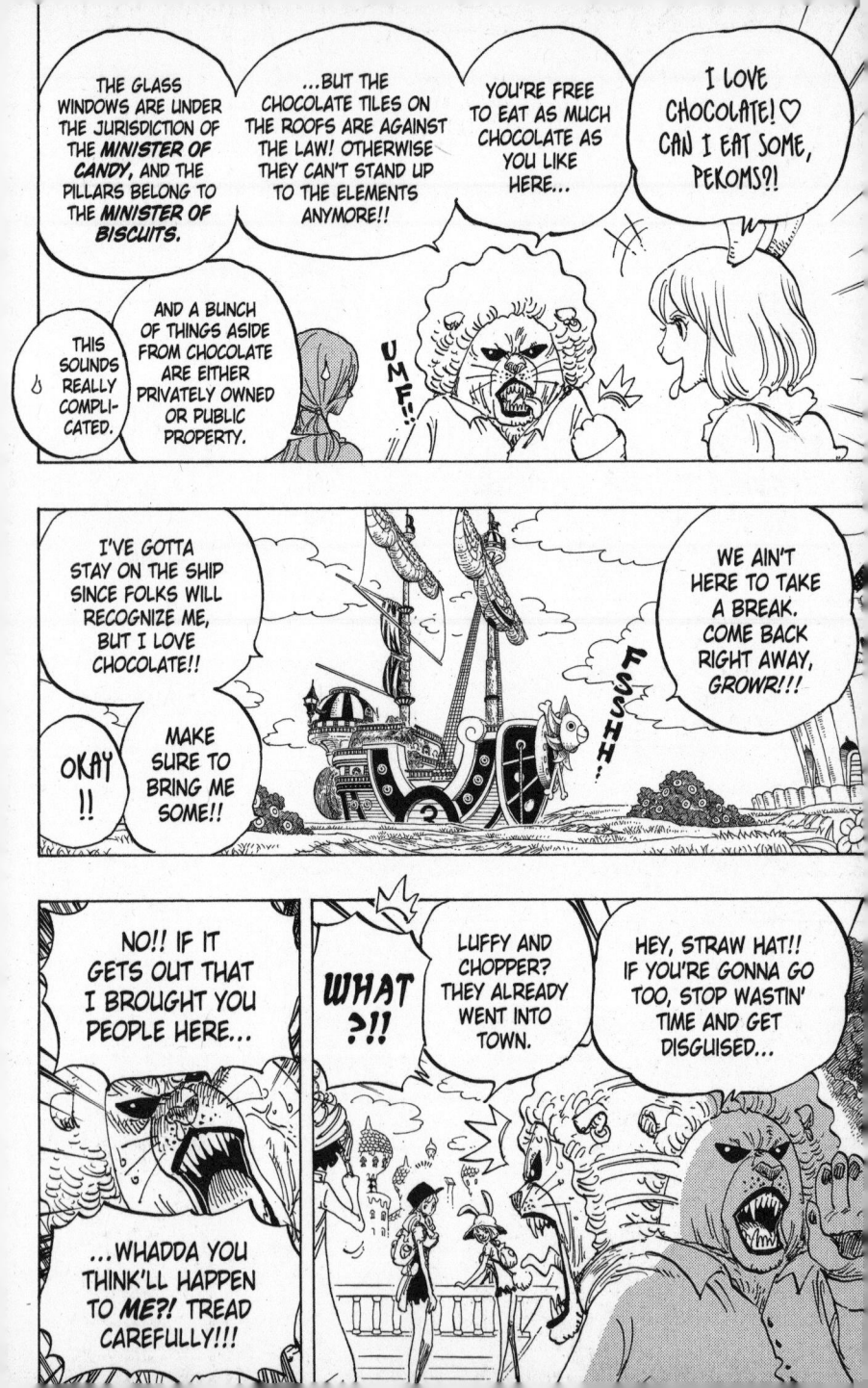
THE GLASS WINDOWS ARE UNDER THE JURISDICTION OF THE MINISTER OF CANDY, AND THE PILLARS BELONG TO THE MINISTER OF BISCUITS.
...BUT THE CHOCOLATE TILES ON THE ROOFS ARE AGAINST THE LAW! OTHERWISE THEY CAN'T STAND UP TO THE ELEMENTS ANYMORE!!
YOU'RE FREE TO EAT AS MUCH CHOCOLATE AS YOU LIKE HERE...
I LOVE CHOCOLATE! ♡ CAN I EAT SOME, PEKOMS?!
THIS SOUNDS REALLY COMPLI-CATED.
AND A BUNCH OF THINGS ASIDE FROM CHOCOLATE ARE EITHER PRIVATELY OWNED OR PUBLIC PROPERTY.
UMF!!
I'VE GOTTA STAY ON THE SHIP SINCE FOLKS WILL RECOGNIZE ME, BUT I LOVE CHOCOLATE!!
OKAY !!
MAKE SURE TO BRING ME SOME!!
TSSHH...
WE AIN'T HERE TO TAKE A BREAK. COME BACK RIGHT AWAY, GROWR!!!
NO!! IF IT GETS OUT THAT I BROUGHT YOU PEOPLE HERE...
...WHADDA YOU THINK'LL HAPPEN TO ME?! TREAD CAREFULLY!!!
WHAT ?!!
LUFFY AND CHOPPER? THEY ALREADY WENT INTO TOWN.
HEY, STRAW HAT!! IF YOU'RE GONNA GO TOO, STOP WASTIN' TIME AND GET DISGUISED...

CAFÉ-EATERS!!!
YOU GOTTA BE KIDDING ME!!!
THEY'RE OVER THERE.
RATTLE
KLAA
RAHH
OH, DON'T WORRY. WE'LL FIND THEM RIGHT AWAY.
CRIN
?

YOU ATE NOT ONLY CHOCOLATE, BUT CANDY, MARSHMALLOWS ...
CHATTER CHATTER
MURMUR MURMUR
THE CHOCOLATE WALLS ARE ONE THING--THEY CAN BE REPLACED LATER!!
BUT YOU ATE THE ENTIRE CAFÉ!!
CHATTER
CHATTER

LISTEN, PAL, THERE'S A REAL GOOD REASON FOR THIS...
I'M HAULING YOU IN!! COME TO THE STATION WITH ME!!!
YOU HAVE COMMITTED THE CRIME OF SNACKALISM OF PRIVATE PROPERTY!!!
CHATTER
CHATTER
BRRP.
...PLUS ALMONDS AND JELLY-BEANS!!
OH?! LET'S HEAR IT!!

IT WAS TOO GOOD TO STOP!!
THAT DOES IT!! YOU IDIOTS ARE COMING WITH ME!!!
YOU'RE UNDER ARREST!!!

CAR-PET ♪
CAR-PET ♪

HMM ?
WAIT, MR. CHOCO-POLICE!
SWOO--SH

WE CAN'T CAUSE A RUCKUS, PEDRO.
OH NO, HE'S ARRESTING THEM!!
KYAA
RAHH

EVEN WORSE!!
HERE'S THE OWNER OF THE CAFÉ!!

OH MY GOOD-NESS!!
JUST LOOK AT THIS!! YOUR BUSINESS...
A FWYING CAWPET!!

OH...IT'S THE CAFÉ OWNER!!
WHOAP!

YOU DIDN'T KEEP YOUR WORD TO ME!!
?!
LOOK HOW MUCH YOU LEFT!!
PUFF!
HON-ESTLY !!
NO. WHO IS THAT?
UM...DO WE KNOW HER?
AND WHAT'S THAT ON HER SHOULDER?
HMM?
?
...WAS A PARTICULAR MASTERPIECE OF MINE!!
ESPECIALLY WHEN THE HARMONY OF JAM, BISCUIT AND CHOCOLATE HERE...
MUR MUR
MUR MUR
UGH
IS IT GOOD?
HERE! EAT UP.♡
!!
CAFÉ CARAMEL OWNER
NITRO THE JELLY
RABIAN THE CARPET

I DID NOT REALIZE THEY WERE DISMANTLING EXPIRED PRODUCTS!!
OH!! PARDON ME, MA'AM!!
YUMMMM
FLOP.
YES, I HIRED THEM TO DO IT!

OH, SO IT WASN'T A CRIME AFTER ALL.
CHATTER
CHATTER

THANK YOU, OFFICER!!
WELL, I'LL LEAVE YOU TO IT!!
I'M SORRY ABOUT THE DISTURBANCE, EVERYONE!!
CHATTER
CHATTER

THERE NEEDS TO BE A SIGN UP WHEN YOU'RE WORKING. THERE WERE STILL CUSTOMERS INSIDE!
YOU'VE GOT TO FOLLOW CODE, BOYS!

THANK YOU!♡
BLUSH♡

DON'T TIRE YOURSELF OUT, WORKING SO HARD WITH THE WEDDING SO NEAR...
WE ALL JUST WANT YOU TO BE HAPPY!!
!
OH, AND... WHILE I HAVE THE CHANCE, MIGHT I ADD...
...CONGRATULATIONS ON YOUR MARRIAGE, LADY PUDDING!

THEY'RE VERY LUCKY.
WHO IS THAT GIRL? SHE'S SO NICE...
LOOKS LIKE SOMEONE STEPPED IN TO SAVE THEM.
YACK
YA...
CHATTER
CHATTER
YO HO HO! THAT'S JUST THE POWER OF THE FUTURE KING OF THE PIRATES!!

WHAT BRINGS YOU--!!
!!
SNA

!!
I HAVEN'T SEEN YOU IN AGES!!
CAPTAIN PEDRO!!

HUH?
CHATTER
CHATTER

I'LL EXPLAIN LATER...
YOU KNOW SOMEONE HERE, PEDRO?!

CHATTER
I'M SIGHT-SEEING. DON'T TELL ANYONE.
OF...OF COURSE! IT'S AN HONOR TO SEE YOU AGAIN!!
CHATTER

THANKS! YOU REALLY SAVED US THERE!!
CHOMP
SO YOUR NAME IS PUDDING!
CHOMP
OHHH...
THAT IT WAS "TOO GOOD TO STOP"!♡
BOO
EEEEK!♡♡
FOR...FOR WHAT YOU SAID!!
HOW COME?!
I'M THE ONE WHO SHOULD BE THANKING YOU!!
OH NO, NOT AT ALL!!
...THEN MIXED IT FOR THREE DAYS AND NIGHTS AT 84 DEGREES!!
I PUT HIGH-PURITY BEET SUGAR INTO THE COCOA BUTTER FOR SWEETNESS, ADDED THE MILK...
DID IT MELT IN YOUR MOUTH PROPERLY?
...IS A NEW RECIPE THAT I DEVISED!
TH-THE CHOCOLATE AT THAT CAFÉ...
EEEK
EEEK
I SWEAR, HEARING THOSE COMPLIMENTS IS GOING TO MAKE ME CRY!!
...
FIDGET FIDGET...

THIS PLACE IS HEAVEN. THE WHOLE TOWN SMELLS LIKE CHOCOLATE!
EVEN THE TABLE IS CHOCOLATE.
I LOVE SWEET STUFF!♡
SO YOU LIKE MAKING CHOCOLATE!!
HEE HEE! I'M GLAD. ♡
WHY, WHAT A SWEET-HEART!!!
NAE

HOW ABOUT A QUICK CUP OF TEA THEN?
TO WASH DOWN ALL THAT SUGAR.
REALLY? THAT'S TOO BAD...
WELL, PUDDING, WE'D LOVE TO SIT AROUND AND THANK YOU PROPERLY...
...BUT WE'RE ACTUALLY IN A HURRY.

...
HUH?!
STOP THAT!!
THE MAN WHO WILL BE KING OF...
OH, I'M LUFFY.
I HAVEN'T HEARD YOUR NAMES YET.
WHOMP!!
BUB
BUB
BUB

WHOLE CAKE ISLAND
HAAA HA HA HA...
MA MA MA MA MA...
DUM-DA-DA♪
HOW MANY MORE DAYS?!
UNTIL THE TEA PARTY?♪
GRRG...
DUM-DAH-♫
HE IS HERE, MAMA!!
AND THE GERMA BOY?
I SEE. ♪
FUR-NY FUR-NY♪
DUM-DA-DA
DUM-DAH-♫
... MAMA!!
THREE DAYS...
FLO-WER FLO-WER♫
WED-DING CAKE! ♫
WED-DING!♪ WED-DING!♪
THE WEDDING CAKE! ♫
HOW ABOUT THE CAKE?!
WED-DING!♪ WED-DING!♫
IT'S A WEDDING !!
DUM-DA-DA♪
DUM-DA-DA♪

ONLY THE FINEST!♪ THROUGH MURDER AND THEFT!♫
GRR-G
GYAA
RAH
AND THE INGREDI-ENTS?
EXTRAVA-GANT! ♪
DUM-DA-DA ♪
AND THE BUDGET?
IT LOOKS JUST FINE!♪
HOW'S THE DESIGN?!
WHEE WHEE
DUM-DA-DA ♪♫
ACQUIRED.
FRUIT! ♫
ACQUIRED.
FLOUR! ♪
ACQUIRED.
EGGS! ♪
THE TEA PARTY FROM HELL!!!
IT'S THE SWEETEST DEAL TO MAKE!♪
LET'S ALL EAT A TASTY CAKE!♫
DUM-DA-DA ♪
SPIN!
SPIN!
DUM-DAH ♫
WE'LL GUARANTEE IT!!!
AND THE TASTE?
RAAH

A DEMONIC SACRIFICE FOR OUR SWEET PASTIME! ♪
IF YOU'RE INVITED, YOU HAVE TO COME!!!
EITHER ONE IS FINE!!
OR SOMEONE'S BLOOD? ♫
IS IT STRAW-BERRY JAM?

OH, I CAN'T WAIT.♪ HE'S HERE, YOU SAY?
DUM-DA-DA♫
DUM-DA-DA♫
HAAAA HA HA HA HA HA... ♫
HE IS HERE! ♫
STRAWWW HAAAT...♪
DO OM!!
A COUNTRY WHERE ALL PEOPLES COME TOGETHER!!!
...LAND OF DREAMS! ♫
THIS IS...
...OUR BELOVED ...
IIIIIT'S... ♪
TOTTO LAND!! ♫

KEY WE'RE PUTTING OUT A MOVIE ON 7.23

★ Yes, it's movie time! *One Piece Film Gold*!! It comes out in Japan on Saturday, July 23, 2016. Is everybody ready for this one? At the time I'm writing this, they're running trailers in theaters and on the home page. Have you seen them yet? It's a two-part promotion. The first trailer features the music of the genius Big Band jazz singer I mentioned last volume, Mayumi Kojima! And the second trailer comes from these fine folks!!

Theme Song: "Give Me Your Anger"

GLIM SPANKY

Did you listen to it? Talk about powerful! We're aiming for a real slick, cool and gorgeous movie this time around, and the music is a crucial part of the atmosphere. I suspect many readers might not be familiar with Glim Spanky yet, but you'll love that awesome singing voice! You'll get chills in the movie theater, I promise! Look forward to it!
Next up, allow me to introduce this fellow!! ⬇

Director: Pit Boss Hiroaki Miyamoto

★ He's the third series director for the *One Piece* TV anime!! A trustworthy man who helmed the ship for six years!! He was a huge help when it came to making the Paramount War as exciting as it should be, and clarifying some of the trickier details of Fish-man Island. He's an expert of the pause, and an entertainer who brings out tears and laughter alike! Let's see what he's got to offer us! Up next is an interview!!

A Comedy Routine from the Director and Executive Producer!

O (Oda): Here's the guy in charge of putting together *Film Gold*! It's our director, Pit Boss Hiroaki Miyamoto!!

M (Miyamoto): Yay! Why am I the pit boss?!

O: Oh, you just seem like you're really in sync with the staff. You're the guy who keeps the team together!

M: Well, if that's the way you meant it, I guess it's all right.

O: So first of all, why do we need to go to the theater to see this? What's wrong with a good old TV?!)≻

M: Why are you mad about it?! Well, a movie and TV show are very different things.

O: Hey, that's just how I felt about it as a kid.

M: I see. Well, first of all, the budget for a movie is much, much different. When you put lots of money into crafting CG, music, big actors, and so on, not only does it enable more creative possibilities, it allows you to take expanded formats like 3-D, 4DX, and MX4D theaters into account while you're producing the movie. This is a film that reaches its greatest potential in the theater!

O: That's right. We're doing this movie in 3-D, 4DX, and MX4D. So it'll pop off the screen! I can't wait to see how we get to fully experience it in person!!

M: And with *Film Gold,* we're actually employing ten times the amount of CG as the previous movie! It's also got the highest number of musical tracks, so we want you to experience all the dynamic camera and sound work on a huge screen with 5.1 surround sound!

O: Gaah, I'm getting so pumped up!! The festival's gonna start!!

M: Yes, it is!! Get hyped with Luffy! Get angry with Luffy! Fight alongside Luffy!!

O: It's a movie you've got to feel for yourself! Come and see it, or I'll throw ya in the clink!!

M: Please don't threaten the audience!!⚡

O: Oh, sorry...

M: Listen, everyone! Come and see this work of entertainment in the theater!!

O: Congrats on finishing up and gaining your freedom!

M: What am I guilty of?⚡ Oh…making a fun movie?

O: Check it out!!

★ Remember what the director just said about all that CG? Well, the people responsible for bringing the gorgeous Gran Tesoro to life are...

Kusanagi

The cutting-edge technicians of the anime world! They've returned after *Film Z* to bring the background of the story into stunning detail again!!

★ Next, we've got some supporting roles to announce. This misfit gang is bringing these kooky characters to the screen!!

Guest Voice Actors!!

Such a stunning lineup! All these people, just for these minor roles?! This is a feat only possible through the deep connections of friendship that *One Piece* has forged through its long run! Thank you all!!

By the way, Hikari Mitsushima, who plays Carina, was once part of the group "Folder 5" that sang one of the *One Piece* anime theme songs! That's beautiful. Welcome back, Hikari!

COMING NEXT VOLUME:

The Straw Hats have faced their share of danger as they've navigated their way through the New World, but they've never met a foe like this! Can they outsmart Big Mom and rescue Sanji from his arranged marriage? Or is it time to start looking for a new cook…?

ON SALE AUGUST 2017!

Love triangle!
Comedic antics!!
Gang warfare?!

A laugh-out-loud story that features a fake love relationship between two heirs of rival gangs!

Story and Art by
NAOSHI KOMI

NISEKOI
False Love

It's hate at first sight...rather, a knee to the head at first sight when **RAKU ICHIJO** meets **CHITOGE KIRISAKI**! Unfortunately, Raku's gangster father arranges a false love match with their rival's daughter, who just so happens to be Chitoge! Raku's searching for his childhood sweetheart from ten years ago, however, with a pendant around his neck as a memento, but he can't even remember her name or face!

AVAILABLE NOW!

NISEKOI © 2011 by Naoshi Komi/SHUEISHA Inc.

BLUE EXORCIST

STORY AND ART BY
KAZUE KATO

THE ORIGINAL MANGA BEHIND THE HIT ANIME!

RAISED BY FATHER FUJIMOTO, A FAMOUS EXORCIST, RIN OKUMURA NEVER KNEW HIS REAL FATHER. ONE DAY A FATEFUL ARGUMENT WITH FATHER FUJIMOTO FORCES RIN TO FACE A TERRIBLE TRUTH – THE BLOOD OF THE DEMON LORD SATAN RUNS IN RIN'S VEINS! RIN SWEARS TO DEFEAT SATAN, BUT DOING THAT MEANS ENTERING THE MYSTERIOUS TRUE CROSS ACADEMY AND BECOMING AN EXORCIST HIMSELF.

Available wherever manga is sold.

www.viz.com

www.shonenjump.com

AO NO EXORCIST © 2009 by Kazue Kato/SHUEISHA Inc.

NARUTO

Story and Art by
Masashi Kishimoto

Naruto is determined to become the greatest ninja ever!

Twelve years ago the Village Hidden in the Leaves was attacked by a fearsome threat. A nine-tailed fox spirit claimed the life of the village leader, the Hokage, and many others. Today, the village is at peace and a troublemaking kid named Naruto is struggling to graduate from Ninja Academy. His goal may be to become the next Hokage, but his true destiny will be much more complicated. The adventure begins now!

WORLD'S BEST SELLING MANGA!

NARUTO © 1999 by Masashi Kishimoto/SHUEISHA Inc.

TEEN
rating.viz.com
SHONEN JUMP
www.shonenjump.com
viz media
www.viz.com

Seraph of the End

VAMPIRE REIGN

STORY BY Takaya Kagami ART BY Yamato Yamamoto

STORYBOARDS BY Daisuke Furuya

Vampires reign—humans revolt!

Yuichiro's dream of killing every vampire is near-impossible, given that vampires are seven times stronger than humans, and the only way to kill them is by mastering Cursed Gear, advanced demon-possessed weaponry. Not to mention that humanity's most elite Vampire Extermination Unit, the Moon Demon Company, wants nothing to do with Yuichiro unless he can prove he's willing to work in a team—which is the last thing he wants!

THE LATEST CHAPTERS SERIALIZED IN WEEKLY SHONEN JUMP

OWARI NO SERAPH © 2012 by Takaya Kagami, Yamato Yamamoto, Daisuke Furuya /SHUEISHA Inc.

59372089740396 FTBC

WORDSOUP OBSOLETE

You're Reading in the Wrong Direction!!

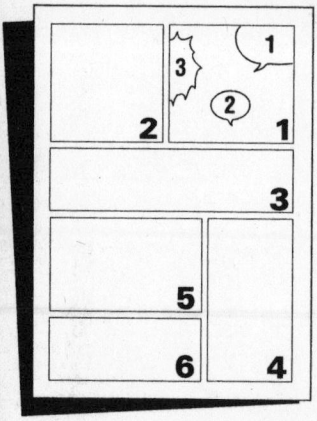

Whoops! Guess what? You're starting at the wrong end of the comic!

...It's true! In keeping with the original Japanese format, **One Piece** is meant to be read from right to left, starting in the upper-right corner.

Unlike English, which is read from left to right, Japanese is read from right to left, meaning that action, sound effects and word-balloon order are completely reversed...something which can make readers unfamiliar with Japanese feel pretty backwards themselves. For this reason, manga or Japanese comics published in the U.S. in English have sometimes been published "flopped"—that is, printed in exact reverse order, as though seen from the other side of a mirror.

By flopping pages, U.S. publishers can avoid confusing readers, but the compromise is not without its downside. For one thing, a character in a flopped manga series who once wore in the original Japanese version a T-shirt emblazoned with "M A Y" (as in "the merry month of") now wears one which reads "Y A M"! Additionally, many manga creators in Japan are themselves unhappy with the process, as some feel the mirror-imaging of their art skews their original intentions.

We are proud to bring you Eiichiro Oda's **One Piece** in the original unflopped format. For now, though, turn to the other side of the book and let the journey begin...!

—Editor